The Unbridgeable Gap:
Blacks and Their Quest for the
American Dream, 1900–1930

The Rand McNally Series on the History of American Thought and Culture

The Unbridgeable Gap: Blacks and Their Quest for the American Dream, 1900-1930

June Sochen
Northeastern Illinois University

Rand McNally & Company • Chicago

The Rand McNally Series on the History of American Thought and Culture

David D. Van Tassel, series editor

To Joyce and Leonard Schrager

Contents

Editor's Preface

In 1870 after the announcement of the final passage of the Fifteenth Amendment to the Constitution, triumphant abolitionists, black and white, gathered in Apollo Hall in New York City where the last meeting of the American Anti-Slavery Society was taking place. Wendell Phillips, president of the society, shared the platform with Lucretia Mott, O. B. Frothingham, Julia Ward Howe, and Frederick Douglas. Although this was a meeting to disband the society, it was a happy not a sad occasion. Frederick Douglas exulted in a hoarse baritone to the jubilant crowd, "I seem to myself to be living in a new world. The sun does not shine as it used to. . . . Not only the slave emancipated, but a personal liberty bill, a civil rights bill, admitted to give testimony in courts of justice, given the right to vote, eligible not only to Congress but to the Presidential chair— and all for a class stigmatized but a little while ago as worthless goods and chattels." Now at last, it seemed, the black man would share the American Dream of liberty and boundless opportunity.

Instead of improving, however, conditions quickly worsened for the black American. In 1881 a southern legislature passed the first of numerous Jim Crow laws, and northerners had begun practicing segregation in a variety of ways. In 1883 the U.S. Supreme Court declared the Civil Rights Act unconstitutional, so that by 1900 a large proportion of black Americans in the South were effectively disfranchised. William Dean Howells observed pessimistically in his novel, *Annie Kilburn*, "I used to think that we had the millennium because slavery was abolished, people have more liberty, but they seem just as far off as ever from justice." The period between 1900 and 1930 presents a curious paradox in the history of the American Dream myth, insofar as it affected black writers and intellectuals. These three decades, on all counts, constitute a nadir in the political, economic, and social condition of black Americans since the end of the Civil War. Yet it is during these very years that the American Dream myth begins to grow and flourish in black literature and periodicals. June Sochen has chosen to make this important theme of the tension between dream and reality central to her general study of black writers and intellectuals, in both North and South, during the first three decades of the twentieth century.

The Unbridgeable Gap, in surveying the thought of black Americans at the beginning of the twentieth century, represents a new departure for the Rand McNally Series on the History of American Thought and Culture. Nevertheless, it fulfills the major purpose of the Series, which is to give students a synthesis, a means of tying together developments in religion, education, philosophy, science, literature and the arts, through a series of short, readable volumes, covering either a broad chronological period or cultural or intellectual themes. Each volume is designed to give a conceptual framework to significant ideas or periods in order to draw together the burgeoning knowledge of the vast area of the American past. The authors are experts in their fields, but they do not represent any one school of social or intellectual history. Each author has chosen his own approach or emphasis, although the general aim is to present ideas in depth and point out the significant relationships between the developments in all areas of intellectual and cultural expression.

In this volume June Sochen presents the results of original research in a brilliant and readable synthesis of the thought and aspirations for black Americans. It is an intellectual history which faces myth with fact, describes the framework and the world view of black thinkers, and in so doing reveals the ways in which the dream myth has shaped the thought of all Americans. This important and thoughtful study demonstrates the continuing power and relevance of the American Dream that will not only inform but challenge every student of modern American society.

DAVID D. VAN TASSEL

Preface

When you place the words "American Dream" next to "black Americans," you immediately create tension. The terms mock each other. The following study is an analysis of the numerous times in which black writers tried to juxtapose these two concepts and arrive at a harmonious marriage. The opening years of this century were years in which life for black Americans changed externally in the sense of movement from rural to city life, and from the South to the North; but they were years in which the underlying attitudes held by white Americans about black people (and blacks about themselves) did not undergo dramatic and extensive changes. Further, they were years in which black intellectuals took on the task of convincing their black compatriots that the words of white America had relevance for them. Black writers and spokesmen, after all, represented the first generation of successful, free black men. And they fervently believed that their experience could be multiplied infinitely. The writings of black Americans during this period rang with excitement, passion, and optimism. Both consciously and unconsciously, they displayed their commitment to the American Dream and to its application to blacks.

The following study is an exercise in intellectual history with a difference. It is an attempt to bring together myth and fact as well as the reality of the intellectual's world with the external reality. While periodical literature provides one major source of material for this study, black fiction and poetry, sociological treatises, as well as factual syntheses have been utilized as well. The life and writings of selected black southerners as well as northerners are included. The attempt to contrast the life and thought of the South to the North provides one of the adventurous themes of this work. Chapters describing the thoughts of black writers alternate with chapters describing the actual life of blacks. Most of the writing on black intellectuals during this period has concentrated upon the Harlem writers of the twenties. The focus of this study, in contrast, is not one group or one section; in this rather brief overview, the hope is to capture the general thought of black writers in both the North and the South on the important subject of the American Dream. As the introductory chapter will describe, this theme received much attention in the black magazines.

A significant portion of this study is based upon a discussion of the periodical literature of the period because it is an excellent barometer of the times and because most black writers first expressed their ideas in the magazines of the day. The magazines, both popular and scholarly (although the emphasis is upon the popular), reflect the concerns, interests, and feelings of American readers. Clearly, everyone, black and white, did not read periodicals. But magazine readership was on the rise during the first thirty years of this century. Further, although it is difficult, if not impossible, to establish the relationship between reading a magazine and personal philosophy, it seems safe to conclude that magazine readers and the people to whom they communicated, shared a set of attitudes and values. In the case of black Americans, for example, the minority of middle and upper class blacks who read *Crisis* and *Opportunity* were often the leaders in their respective communities; surely, they were influenced by the thinking of a W. E. B. DuBois and tried to influence their followers in turn.

The terms in which the magazine writers discussed the "Negro problem" are also revelatory. The vocabulary used, the descriptions rendered, and the definition of the solutions all provide great insights into the thoughts and values of white America as well as black America. Thus, a review of periodical literature tells us who were the leading writers on this subject in the periodical field as well as their views and estimations of the situation. This is, of course, a selective study. Every black writer is not included. One rule of thumb used by the author was the frequency of articles written by a particular writer as found in the periodical indices. Another was the inclusion of the major black fiction writers of the period as viewed by their contemporaries.

Attention is primarily given to the following black periodicals: *Crisis, Opportunity,* the *Southern Workman,* and the *Messenger.* These journals were selected as representative of black writing as well as the best of their genre. Although the American Dream theme is the central concern of this study, attention is also given to some of the black spokesmen who rejected the validity or applicability of the American Dream for black Americans. I must hastily add, however, that I consider this group to be a very small minority of a minority (those blacks writing on the subject at all). For, and now I am anticipating myself, one of my conclusions is that the dream myth permeated most of black literature of the period. And most black spokesmen, either consciously or unconsciously, were articulators of the American Dream motif. In fact, by looking at the rejectors of the dream, and their reasons for repudiating it, additional insight can be obtained on the strengths and weaknesses of the dream myth in America.

The chapter entitled "1930" surveys the way in which many leading black intellectuals responded to the Depression and how they related the economic disaster to basic American values. "A Final View" tries to relate the potency of the dream mythology to the American reform tradition and speculatively consider some of the broader implications of this study. All in all, *The Unbridgeable Gap* tries to describe the framework and the world view of black thought during the first thirty years of this century. The importance and power of the American Dream and its attending value system has played a vital role in shaping all of our thought. This study reveals how the myth of the dream reflected black intellectual thought and how, by implication, its relevance and force still obtain today.

I would like to take this opportunity to express my gratitude to my graduate assistant, Mrs. Paula Pfeffer, whose research aid was a great help in the preparation of this book.

June Sochen

Fall, 1971

**The Unbridgeable Gap:
Blacks and Their Quest for the
American Dream, 1900–1930**

Chapter 1

Introduction

Webster's New World Dictionary defines a myth as "a story that recounts purportedly historical events to explain how traditions, major doctrines, religions, and similar nuclear concepts arose." In the United States a myth has been developed to describe the unique life opportunities available to and for all. The American Dream myth, which is composed of religious and secular components, provides all children as well as newcomers with a value system, a history, and a rationale. Since colonial times, Americans have learned that this continent, settled by good, God-fearing people, provides a unique opportunity to build a great society—a society that meets both man's and God's stringent requirements for success. From John Winthrop to Benjamin Franklin to Horatio Alger to Illinois Senator Charles Percy, Americans have learned from their parents and their teachers that this rich land, rich in natural resources and human aspiration, provides infinite means of pursuing happiness and obtaining material rewards.

The ethic of individual hard work, thrift, and discipline, commonly known as the Protestant ethic, is one crucial ingredient of the American Dream mythology. Infinite opportunity in this rich, never ending land is another. Father Hennepin, a French explorer in the seventeenth century, observed the immense wealth of the

1

North American continent. Whitefish larger than carp, numerous deer, flocks of wild turkey, and fertile lands encircling fresh water lakes were all admired by the early pioneer. His report has been substantiated frequently ever since. Couple this observation with the idea of progress and you have another component of the American Dream. Individual effort expended in honest work will inevitably lead to progress in this best of all promised lands.* Thus, the richness of the natural scene and the Protestant ethic combined to form the basis for the dream. Human and material progress as well as the continuous possibility of mobility became the forceful faith of Americans.

In the first thirty years of this century, the period under study in this book, the American Dream myth was alive and vibrant. Despite our involvement in the First World War and the decade of the twenties ending in a cataclysmic depression, Americans clung stubbornly to the belief that America was the land of opportunity and that each one of us could succeed in this rich environment. Economic problems pointed to some weaknesses in the system—but they were surely able to be corrected. Intellectuals during this period viewed political democracy as obtainable also (once you removed the corrupt scoundrels from office and allowed for initiative, referendum, and recall). If the good life could not be obtained here, they reasoned, where else could freedom and opportunity be gained? There were no real contenders for the faith.

The years 1900 to 1930 saw the first vigorous articulation of this myth by black Americans. A forceful, dynamic black leadership and set of organizations had developed by the early 1900s. The NAACP, Urban League, and the Booker T. Washington Organization were all founded upon the values and goals of the American Dream. With very few exceptions that will be treated later, these organizations stood for and their leaders expressed, often eloquently, their faith in the American Dream and the possibility of its goals being

---

* The literature on the American Dream is extensive and various. See, for example, Irvin G. Wyllie, *Self-Made Man in America* (New York: Free Press, 1966); Howard Mumford Jones, *The Pursuit of Happiness* (Cambridge, Mass.: Harvard University Press, 1953); and John Morton Blum, *The Promise of America* (New York: Houghton Mifflin, 1966). Further, the idea of the American Dream is intertwined with the idea of the uniqueness of America which also has a long history beginning with John Winthrop's "for wee must consider that wee shall be as a Citty upon a Hill, the eies of all people are uppon us."

fulfilled for black Americans. Indeed, the viability of the dream was often viewed *in terms* of black Americans. Whether the myth of American opportunity was real or ephemeral would be determined by its validity for black Americans. This theme was iterated and reiterated by black American spokesmen. As one black writer put it, "To many students it sometimes appears as if the Negro would be the rock upon which the good ship Democracy will founder unless more judgment and common sense is shown by the people in the pilot-house."[1]

After all, who was more American than black Americans? In an age of mass immigration, of foreign-looking and -sounding people crowding into urban America, who represented one of the oldest native groups? "This land is ours by right of birth," James Weldon Johnson reminded black Americans.

> This land is ours by right of toil;
> We helped to turn its virgin earth
> Our sweat is in its fruitful soil.[2]

If America was the chosen land, then black Americans surely had to be one of its chosen people. During slavery, this claim, of course, could not be made. But 1900 was thirty-five years after the Civil War and a generation after the proper constitutional amendments had been passed to insure the black man's status as an American. Black Christian ministers frequently compared their followers to the Hebrews; just as the ancient Hebrews had been enslaved and then freed, so had black Americans. Further, according to this view, both groups had been chosen to suffer and would eventually be rewarded for their travail. For those who wanted to redirect black Americans' thoughts from the next world to this world, the theme of the chosen could be interpreted to mean the exceptionality of Americans, with black Americans being an authentic and significant group. The freed black man, in this free land, could reap the rewards open to all men in America.

Thus, it was possible to interpret the black man's experience in

---

[1] A. L. Jackson, "The Negro's Aspirations," *Forum* 65 (February, 1921): 217.

[2] James Weldon Johnson, "The Larger Success," *Southern Workman* 52 (September, 1923): 431.

America within the American Dream motif. If this was the land of opportunity, of mobility, of progress for its citizens, then black Americans must be included, as they were among the nation's oldest residents. If Americans were special people who would be rewarded in this land of abundance, then black Americans, already convinced of their special role as sufferers, could hopefully believe that speciality may have some earthly gifts attached to it also. If hard work, individual effort, sacrifice, and self-discipline were American virtues essential to the fulfillment of the dream, they were virtues known to black Americans. However, never had these virtues paid off before. The rewards had not existed for slaves. But now, thirty-five years out of slavery, black American leaders were telling their people that the words, the goals, and the faith of America pertained to them. As of the twentieth century, blacks, the message said, were to be included in the American Dream.

This view provided a powerful challenge to the white advocates of the American Dream as well as to the black American leaders. By confronting white America with her own words and goals, black Americans were asking: How valid is your dream? To whom does it apply? Is it real for anyone except white Anglo-Saxon Protestants? And the white spokesmen for the dream, caught in their own rhetoric, were forced to acknowledge its application to all, at the same time wondering if, in fact, it ever meant what it said. Words such as "all men are created equal" have a great deal of power, drama, and grandeur attached to them. But even the creator of those words, Thomas Jefferson, recognized from the beginning that they expressed more of a hope than a reality. In the twentieth century, the American group that was most glaringly excluded from those words demanded that they become real. The piper either had to be paid or the promise had to be revised. During the 1900–1930 period, the hope persisted that the words would become a reality and that America would live up to her own ideals.

The American Dream rhetoric is uncompromising. Equality and its implementation, if these words are ruthlessly enforced, lead to the destruction of all superstructures built upon heredity, wealth, and discrimination. It only recognizes a hierarchy built upon talent, training, and discipline. In fact, the Jeffersonian ideal of an aristocracy of ability and education more closely fulfills the belief in equality; this goal, admittedly never practiced in human society, allows for all people to work, to develop their potential, and to be rewarded for their accomplishments. Equality of opportunity, in a land of opportunity, has become the acceptable way of interpreting the egalitarian ideal of the Declaration of Independence. In practice, this means that all of the institutions of society must be equally open to all of the nation's citizens. All schools, voting polls, factories, churches, and recreational facilities must be available to all people; and the same standards of judgment must obtain for all too. If a person does not get a college education or a government job, it must be because, given the same basic opportunities as anyone else, he did not qualify—and not because of his color or his background which predetermined his failure. Black American writers, during the early years of this century, continuously pleaded for the implementation of Jefferson's goal.

Many white intellectuals also were discovering, much to their amazement, that conditions which they assumed had been naturally developed were in fact the result of environmental, changeable conditions. Sociologists such as Lester Frank Ward, for example, noted that human beings often suffered because of blocked opportunities, discriminatory treatment, and a ruthless suppression of unskilled labor. Man, then, rather than being inevitably determined by his genetic makeup, played a role in his own destiny. But also, individual man in urban and industrialized America could not succeed by himself. Collectivity, rather than individuality, became the watchword of Progressive intellectuals like Herbert Croly and Walter Weyl. Rather than accepting the view of Yale professor William Graham Sumner that government could not ameliorate social conditions because it would upset the balance of nature, intellectuals and activists began to consider the possibility of changing environmental conditions in order to solve social evils.

Many white liberal intellectuals had discovered, in other words, that the Jeffersonian ideal of openness and equal opportunity for all had been obstructed, if not denied. Their job, as they saw it, was to reopen the channels of opportunity, to reassert the validity of the American Dream. The freedom to achieve, the hope for success, and the abundant environment still obtained in America. But its free access to all of its citizens had been shut off by governmental favoritism to big industry, by corruption in high places, and by the violent repression of unorganized labor by big business. Thus, many intellectuals (known as Progressives), settlement house workers, sociologists, and journalists of the *New Republic* and

Nation sort, joined hands with the articulate black leadership to renew the faith and reality of American values.

This, then, became the partnership that tried to dramatize to white America the tremendous significance of making the American Dream real for black Americans. To Oswald Garrison Villard, publisher of the *Nation,* to Jane Addams, noted settlement house leader, and to Mary White Ovington, a reporter, it became a mission to revitalize and realize the dream of America. But to the black participants, who staffed the organizations created in the 1910s to deal with gaining civil rights for Negroes, and who contributed so much of the journalistic literature on the subject, it was a crusade to right the specific wrongs suffered by black Americans. The black intellectuals knew that they could not achieve any success without the cooperation and aid of whites; the white intellectuals were ideologically committed and with their help, the black leaders hoped to gain the support of important portions of the white population. The concreteness of the problem, as seen by the black intelligensia, made it more than a desire to recapture the truth and beauty of abstract American values. The grim life-style of the poor blacks in rural Georgia, the terror of lynching, the unfulfilled promises in the already forming ghettos of the North, and the stark experiences of discrimination which every black American personally knew about made it an extremely immediate and forceful issue.

But the irony of the whole matter was that the black leaders were also captives of the dream. They wanted to believe, and they did believe, that it could apply to their black brothers. They devoted their lives to making it a realizable dream, a dream that could be attained. The methods, means, goals, and world view that they expressed reflected their implicit commitment to the same dream that had motivated white Americans for years to work hard, save their money, go to school, and advance up the socioeconomic ladder. During this period, black writers believed that these goals were valid and they pointed enthusiastically to the progress of black Americans to substantiate their faith; at the same time, however, they noted the vicious discrimination against blacks in the job market, in housing, and in education. Although progress, as Eugene Kinckle Jones, the executive secretary of the Urban League in the twenties noted, was inevitable, there were detours and rocky paths that black Americans had to negotiate.

Often, in order to soften the unmanageable dilemma, black writers focused upon the South as the section most guilty of violating American principles and they tried to get white northerners to reform their southern brothers. But this tactic, which had failed during Reconstruction, did not enjoy any success during this period either.

The task of black writers was often a double and difficult one: they found that at the same time that they tried to appeal to the white man's conscience to live up to his stated ideals, they had to convince many blacks that the ideals did, in fact, apply to them. In this sense, the black writers played the role of articulator and propagandist for the American Dream to black America. Clearly, most whites who understood the subversive quality of the egalitarian dream would not preach it to their black brothers. Even without direct preaching, however, black America had been hearing the myth and rhetoric for many years. They had never believed that it spoke to them. And, in this sense, they were right. Now it was the task of the black intellectuals to convince the black masses that it did include them and that despite their negative experiences whenever they tried to obtain equality, they should continue trying.

Black writers never tired of citing statistics that demonstrated the increase in property ownership, the lowering of the illiteracy rate, and the improvement in health of black Americans. This information was designed to convince white Americans that blacks were indeed helping themselves and willfully improving their living conditions. But another significant function of this type of data was to raise the morale of discouraged or disillusioned blacks. It is only when you read black writings written exclusively for a black audience that you see the propaganda efforts at work. It was in the pages of *Crisis*, the NAACP journal, of *Opportunity*, the organ of the Urban League, and of the *Southern Workman*, the magazine of Hampton Institute, that the reader comes to appreciate the efforts of black intellectuals to convince their own people of the viability of the dream. Direct efforts to inculate the virtues and values of the Protestant ethic and of white Anglo-Saxon Americanism are frequently described in the black periodicals of the period. Horatio Alger success stories are reported in every issue; examples of the black man's concrete progress and success become constant reminders as well as encouragements to black readers that they, too, can become part of the mobile, advancing portion of the American population. The slave experience and its heritage of discouragement and distrust of whites had to be overcome. Black Americans, properly equipped with a good education, self-discipline, a clean shirt, and a good Christian demeanor could succeed in America. This was the central message articulated by black writers for their black audiences. And in this period, many people persistently believed that it was being realized.

In the "white" magazines, the black writers tried to impress their audiences with the real gains made by black Americans. They gave statistics, presented case studies, and generally wrote in terms of the American politico-economic framework. The American Dream motif was the one within which they operated. Their main chore and goal were to convince their white readers that black Americans were inherently the same as they were. Blacks dreamed the same dreams, strove for the same ideals, and generally lived their lives according to the same rule book. The tragedy they continually referred to was the white unwillingness to permit black Americans equal opportunity to fulfill the dream.

The opening years of this century saw the Progressive mentality grab hold of white and black reformers. Progress, of course, was very much within the framework of the American Dream. In the early twentieth century, it was interpreted to mean the rational solution of all the new problems emanating from industrialization and the happy entry of all Americans into the nirvana of American abundance. The methodology of American reformers, methods that had been traditionally employed in American history to deal with her problems, were utilized: the power of persuasion through the press, appeals to conscience, friendly pressure upon governmental authorities, the power of the ballot box, and the passage of ameliorative laws. It was fervently believed that the enactment of a favorable law, for example, the Dyer Anti-Lynching Law, would effectively eliminate the problem for which it was designed. More significantly perhaps in this particular time period, the implementation and enforcement of *existing* constitutional amendments became the primary focus of much black writing and effort. If the Thirteenth, Fourteenth, and Fifteenth Amendments were heeded, respected, and obeyed, argued many black spokesmen, the American Dream would be a reality. Of course they were right but they found it difficult to convince, let alone force, white America to obey her own laws.

Black American spokesmen discovered that the reform tools were only partially available to them. The press, for example, did not provide frequent coverage of stories dealing with black America. White newspapers only dealt with crises, such as race riots, but did not provide regular news features on the accomplishments or problems of black America. Chicago Negroes had to read the Chicago *Defender* to find out about their neighbors' activities. Because prominent black men were few in terms of power positions, the newspapers accurately reflected the fact that the power elite of America did not include many representatives of black Americans (or any minority group for that matter). The magazines provided more information about the Negro but did not write in urgent tones imploring readers to action. Often, the magazine articles dealt with Negro music or inspirational examples of successful black Americans. Only the black writers adopted voices of urgency to dramatize the depths of the problem. Most white Americans, if newspaper and magazine topics are any reflection, did not want to be presented with messages demanding them to act, to change their behavior, to donate money to worthy causes, or in general to alter their habitual frame of reference.

The federal government was hardly more friendly to the gestures and pleas of civil rights advocates. Woodrow Wilson sanctioned segregation in Washington; Theodore Roosevelt was sorry he had dinner with Booker T. Washington; Warren G. Harding advocated civil rights for Negroes but certainly not social equality; and the southern bloc in Congress prevented any meaningful reform legislation for black Americans. Thus, black writers found that the traditional means of accomplishing change in America were not readily available to them. But this fact did not stop them from using the very same methods continuously. Indeed, the persistence of black writers to utilize American tools of reform and to advocate the fulfillment of the American Dream is the greatest testimony to the power and allure of the dream.

The problem of race relations, however, was not seen in those years (is it now?) as the double chore of convincing blacks and whites that the dream related to black people. By speaking to the need for enforcement of existing laws as well as to the inherent cause of justice to all embodied in the Declaration of Independence, the writers and propagandists for the American Dream *assumed* the acceptance of the rhetoric but knew in their hearts (but ignored the fact) that the rhetoric was not believed by either race. Black writers provided some evidence to support their case for progress but, once again, they knew that their evidence dealt with the minority, with the exceptions, and not the majority. And the majority, both black and white, did not believe the black Horatio Alger stories applied to all blacks; and, of course, they were right. As the discussion in the following chapter suggests, the gap between the words and the actions was enormous.

Chapter 2

Inculcating the Dream: The "Southern Workman" and Reality

How would black southerners learn of the American Dream? Who would expose them to the possibilities of life as free men in America? Black schools, largely supported by white philanthropy, became one major propaganda agency for the American Dream in the South. Hampton Institute of Virginia best exemplifies this effort. Founded during the Reconstruction by General Samuel Armstrong, a man much admired by the school's most famous graduate, Booker T. Washington, its curriculum emphasized self-help and training blacks in agriculture and the vocations. Economic independence became the major goal, a goal which, it was implicitly assumed, would lead inevitably to full participation in American life. Emphasis was placed upon technical skills and not classical ones. The student body, composed largely of farmers' sons, were taught scientific use of the land as well as usable skills. This educational program, of course, fit in neatly with the white southerners' view of the capabilities of black men. Blacks, according to the overwhelming majority of white Americans, were not able to study

11

Greek, Latin, and other high-flown subjects and therefore should not be exposed to them. One visitor to Hampton Institute in 1893 offered the cautionary advice that education for blacks should not raise their expectations because their hopes would only be dashed in America.

Hampton Institute, however, did offer classical subjects for some of its students. When Madame Blanc, the French novelist mentioned above,* saw black girls studying Greek, she was appalled. "I consider," she wrote later, "the classes in sewing, cooking and laundry work established by good General Armstrong more useful."[1] If the blacks were given limited, vocational education, they would remain in their proper station in life; classical, liberal arts education raised their hopes and was therefore undesirable. This opinion was surely shared by the majority of southern and northern whites.

Given this frame of reference, it is interesting to note how positive and forceful the *Southern Workman,* the publication of Hampton Institute, was in inculcating the American Dream myth into its readers. Hampton Institute, after all, was the model school for blacks in the South, and the South, during this whole period, was the home of the majority of American blacks. Thus, the views of its magazine both reflected and influenced black thinking. To the editors of the magazine, American values were also the property of black Americans. After all, what other values or virtues could be taught to rural black Americans trying to adjust to a semi-free status? But, and this certainly was ironic and tragic, the goals of the American Dream *did* raise hopes, *did* demand evidence of fulfillment, and therefore *did* create frustrations. Madame Blanc appreciated this fact. She wanted to avoid the problem by not pretending that black Americans were equal to whites, by not pretending that blacks were equally educable and equally entitled to the rewards of American diligence and hard work. But neither the editors nor the contributors to *Southern Workman* accepted Madame Blanc's first premise nor did they accept her con-

---

* Madame Blanc wrote numerous novels as well as travelogues. She visited this country a few times; one of her volumes was entitled *The Condition of Woman in the United States.* It was in this book that she discussed Negro education in the South.

[1] Madame Blanc, *The Condition of Woman in the United States,* trans. Abby Langdon Alger (Boston: Roberts Brothers, 1895), p. 281.

clusion. The contributors to the magazine, often the leading black spokesmen of the period, vigorously expressed their belief in the progressive ability of blacks to improve their lot. The implicit assumption in much of their writing also was that each black man had a measure of control over his own destiny. If he worked hard, took pride in his efforts, and persevered, he would reap the benefits of his labor.

There is a major paradox evident in the position of the black writers for this magazine and indeed in much of the writing of the period: that is, they are aware of the external conditions and circumstances that prevent equal opportunity for black Americans at the same time that they urge blacks to try harder, work longer, and take pains to improve themselves. If white southerners, for example, institutionalized the inferior position of the black in every facet of life, then no matter how hard the black man tried, he was doomed in advance. But black writers, although apparently aware of the grim reality, still spoke within the individualistic framework of the dream myth—while white America collectively obstructed individual efforts from being rewarded. When reading the *Southern Workman*, one is convinced that individuals, no matter what their color is, control their own destiny. The American view of individualism and egalitarianism pervaded the magazine's pages.

Some examples are appropriate to illustrate this point. First, the word progress appears frequently in the titles of articles as well as in the content of the articles.[2] Individual progress of outstanding black men was cited and discussed frequently. "An Upward Climb" described the success story of Robert S. Abbott, the publisher of the Chicago *Defender* and a Hampton Institute graduate. Readers were encouraged to follow in the footsteps of this black Horatio Alger story.[3] Commencement speeches at the institute were regularly reprinted in the *Southern Workman;* they always displayed an inspirational tone urging the new graduates to practice the virtues of

---

[2] "Fifty Years of Negro Progress," January, 1913; "The Rise and Progress of Manual Training," January, 1902; "Negro Schools and Educational Progress in the South," November, 1908; "Fundamentals of Race Progress," December, 1921; "The Larger Success," September, 1923; and "Educational Achievements and Needs," April, 1929, are a few illustrations of the title articles from *Southern Workman* that exemplify this idea.

[3] Unsigned article, "An Upward Climb," *Southern Workman* 50 (September, 1921): 409–12.

America and assured them that the rewards would naturally follow. The table of contents of each issue confirmed the editors' commitment to the American framework and the American belief in progress based upon individual effort and accomplishment.

Coupled with this theme and often interwoven with it was the emphasis upon racial pride and self-help. This idea was not antagonistic to the American Dream motif. Rather, it was seen as part of it. In a real sense, the true meaning of black power was articulated in the 1920s in the pages of the *Southern Workman*. Black pride and power according to this interpretation, meant economic, educational, and cultural independence. The American ideal of liberty and equal opportunity allowed for the achievement of the first two goals, and the American belief in toleration provided the fulfillment of the last one. Ethnic pluralism, in other words, although not expressed in this way, became the goal of black Americans. As Carter G. Woodson, the noted black historian, said, "... liberty is to come to the Negro, not as a bequest, but as a conquest." The black American had to work actively to achieve his success. "We must cease trying to straighten our hair," Woodson said, "and bleach our faces, and be Negroes—and be good ones."[4]

All of the writers in this magazine, and this point cannot be stressed too vigorously, were respectable middle-class blacks, who had achieved a measure of success through hard work, education, and perseverance. Their lives, therefore, were personal models to their students and readers. Dependent black slaves had to be transformed into independent black men. In order to do this, they had to be indoctrinated with an ideology, a dream that would inspire them to action, and that would be realizable, at least for some of them. The American Dream applied to black men served this purpose. The American goals of individual success based upon a foundation of racial pride enabled blacks to learn their own history, preserve their own culture, and yet receive a measure of participation and integration, if you will, into the American system. Economic and educational aims had to be accomplished within the white American context but cultural independence could be developed in a parallel manner.

---

[4] Carter G. Woodson, "Some Things Negroes Need to Do," *ibid.* 51 (January, 1922): 33–6.

"Every teacher in a colored school is a missionary," claimed one writer.[5] The educators had to teach racial pride and help the students develop a positive self-image. After all, self-confidence is one of the significant foundation points for success in the American environment. Success cannot be achieved unless you believe in yourself and your ability to perform effectively. Thus, black history had to be taught to black children. They had to become acquainted with the positive accomplishments of their people in American history. All of this sounds remarkably contemporary, yet these views were written in the twenties, and not in Harlem, but in Virginia.

> All this is by way of reminding ourselves that for two genera-
> tions we have given brown and black children a blonde ideal
> of beauty to worship, a milk-white literature to assimilate, and
> a pearly Paradise to anticipate, in which their dark faces would
> be hopelessly out of place.[6]

Education was often viewed as the single most significant factor in securing the denied social change.[7] Once again, this notion is very much a part of the American ideology; the way to improve people's ability to earn a living, the way to eliminate prejudice and poverty, and the way to solve all social ills is to provide education for all. The school has been, and continues to be, the institution that is required to assimilate foreigners, to elevate ambitions, and to tame passions. Thus, the Reverend Reverdy C. Ransom, a black Social Gospel minister, advised farmers, preachers, and teachers at a conference at Hampton Institute to encourage the exceptional child, to offer good education for all, and to try to obtain greater funds for black schools. He compared the southern black child to the immigrant child in the North and said that they faced the same educational problem of adjustment.[8] The comparison of the southern rural black child to the newly arrived urban immigrant

---

[5] Alice Dunbar-Nelson, "Negro Literature for Negro Pupils," *ibid.* (February, 1922): 61.

[6] *Ibid.*, p. 59.

[7] See for example "The Rise and Progress of Manual Training" and "Negro Schools and Educational Progress in the South," mentioned earlier.

[8] Reverdy C. Ransom, "Educational Problems," *ibid.* 50 (September, 1921): 417–20.

demonstrates Ransom's belief that the similarities between these two groups were greater than the differences; both were assimilable; and both could be absorbed into the American mainstream with the proper education. Race as the significant dividing line is not acknowledged, thus displaying the reverend's implicit assumption that prejudice and discrimination were based upon ignorance (on both sides). When Italian children learned English, adopted American middle-class manners, and observed the Protestant ethic, they would succeed. Ransom suggested that the same path would reap the same results for southern blacks.

Other contributors to the magazine pointed to the decrease in illiteracy, a statistic frequently referred to in all of the journal literature, to demonstrate the progress being made by blacks to raise their educational level.[9] The 1900 census claimed that 50 percent of black Americans could read while fifty years earlier only 10 percent could. By 1920, only 22.9 percent of the Negroes over ten were illiterate. The fact that more black children were going to school and learning how to read, that more were continuing their education (the number of black colleges increased from 31 schools in 1916 to 77 in 1926) confirmed the black educators' commitment to education. By the end of the twenties, under twenty thousand blacks were in black colleges—not enough to equal the talented tenth quota advocated by the northern black intellectual, W. E. B. DuBois. But once again, progress, in educational terms as well as economic terms, is relative. Considering the status of blacks under slavery and the fact that a decade was not viewed as an interminably long time period, the results seemed impressive. In the South, this was especially true. While 62 percent of the white children went to school in 1920, 46.4 percent of the black children did also. The gap between the races, at least in educational matters, seemed to be narrowing.

The fact that southern legislators appropriated one-tenth as much money for black education as white education did not escape the notice and constant comment of black writers. But how did you convince white southerners, with a deep reluctance to raise taxes for public education for *anyone*, to increase their allotment for

---

[9] Dr. Sara W. Brown, "Fundamentals of Race Progress," *ibid.* (December, 1921): 538–44; and J. S. Dickerman, "Negro Literacy and Illiteracy," *ibid.* 31 (September, 1902): 473–76.

black children whom they deemed uneducable? Indeed, this was a question that black southerners could never answer to their own satisfaction. The *Southern Workman* pointed out that unjust discrepancy, lamented its existence, and asked, through its most articulate spokesmen, for the moral, upstanding members of the white southern community to rectify this great social wrong. The statistical evidence demonstrated conclusively that for every dollar spent to educate black children, ten dollars was spent for white children. Contrary to the American faith, presenting the evidence did not inevitably lead to a correction of the situation.

The optimism, indeed, often the sheer buoyancy, with which many black writers described the educational improvements and possibilities fills the reader with incredulity. For example, in 1902 while describing manual training schools in the South for blacks (and this was, after all, the major type of educational institution available), one writer commented that the goal of manual education was materialistic but he found spiritual meaning in it. "Whenever I step into a room where the manual training idea is being carried out—no matter how poorly—I have the feeling of being in a consecrated place."[10] Another eductional propagandist believed that the progress made in white southern education would spread into black schools. A liberal spirit, combined with constructive efforts at black-white cooperation, and increased appropriations would result in progress. "And although but few of the Negro schools are near the front of the column of progress, yet a large number are struggling forward."[11] A third writer attributed the prosperity in the Black Belt of Florida in 1908 to the Florida State Normal and Industrial School.[12] *Southern Workman* writers used words such as "uplift," "progress," "moving ahead," and "forward" frequently. They continuously and consistently pointed to education as one of the chief means of bringing black men into the mainstream of American life and opportunity.

Articles on education frequently observed that Julius Rosenwald, a white northern philanthropist and founder of Sears, Roebuck

---

[10] Arthur U. Craig, "The Rise and Progress of Manual Training," *ibid.* 31 (January, 1902): 33.

[11] W. T. B. Williams, "Negro Schools and Educational Progress in the South," *ibid.* 37 (November, 1908): 626.

[12] W. H. A. Howard, "In the Black Belt of Florida," *ibid.* (May, 1908): 284–90.

and Company, provided a good deal of the schoolhouses for black students. One source stated that one out of every five rural black schools was a Rosenwald school and thirty-five percent of all black school children in the rural South went to a Rosenwald school.[13] One conclusion, therefore, seemed to be that northern white financial support, privately sought and given, was a more effective means of obtaining education money than appeals to southern politicians and citizens.

The subject of politics was conspicuously absent from the pages of the *Southern Workman.* Economic self-sufficiency, developing independence, encouraging racial pride, and obtaining an education were acceptable subjects, not dangerous ones. They did not produce "uppity niggers." They did not encourage rebelliousness and/or insolence. Hampton Institute and the magazine's editors, as has already been suggested, understood the white southern culture in which they operated. They appreciated the cultural imperatives which demanded that they do not threaten or challenge in any way the basic white supremacy structure of the society.* The editors of the *Southern Workman* respected and feared this framework. They lived in the South, wanted to see some concrete progress made for their black brothers, and knew that even minimal accomplishments could not be made if they were accused of being subversive or aggressive.

Thus, developing agricultural skills and learning vocations did not pose a serious challenge to the status quo and it was permitted. Economic progress, as important a theme in the pages of the *Southern Workman* as educational progress, received much attention. Even if the progress was modest, if not miniscule, writers commented on it. Witness this discussion of farmers in the South, based upon information from the census of 1900:

> Of course it is to be borne in mind that these farms of the Negroes are generally very small, especially as compared with those of the whites, often containing no more than two or three acres, and this perhaps in a swamp or pine barren where the

---

[13] S. L. Smith, "Negro Public Schools in the South," *ibid.* 57 (November, 1928): 448–61.

* Due to restrictive and discriminatory laws such as the white primary, literacy tests and the grandfather clause, the Democratic party in the South prevented blacks from voting.

ground is so poor as to be called almost worthless. Yet even in such cases, the actual ownership of a piece of real estate with the most modest improvements, signifies a great advance over a condition of absolute penury.[14]

Indeed, possession of private property for former slaves did signal an advance, however small the acreage of property. The measuring stick of progress remained the traditional white American one of an individual freehold of land.

Failure to acquire land was often viewed as personal, individual failure. References were made to the masses of rural Negroes as being shiftless and ignorant, inferring therefore that the individual Negro had control over his own person and future if he so desired. "It is only necessary to say," observed one author, "that there is not one single restriction placed upon the Delta Negro in the matter of acquiring land, there being neither discrimination as to price nor prejudice as to color."[15] And in another sphere of economic activity, young women were told that domestic service was dignified and important work. "There is no reason why a woman of character, graciousness, and skill should not make her work as a domestic as respectable and as highly regarded as the work of a girl behind a department store counter."[16] Thus, discussions of economic opportunity as well as examples of individual economic success confirmed the very American value of judging success and failure in individualistic terms, ignoring entirely the social aspects of both.

The oppressiveness of life in the South for the majority of black Americans did not receive any attention in the pages of the *Southern Workman*. The editors presented a cheery countenance, a symbol of great hope and infinite endurance. They never advocated leaving. They lived in the South and tried to transfer the white Anglo-Saxon Protestant philosophy to southern black Protestants. They expressed the firm belief that life for blacks in the South could be comfortable. If the American Dream had been con-

---

[14] G. S. Dickerman, "Tenure Farms in the South," *Southern Workman* 32 (January, 1903): 46.

[15] Alfred Holt Stone, "The Negro Farmer in the Mississippi Delta," *ibid.* (October, 1903): 460.

[16] Fannie Barrier Williams, "The Problem of Employment for Negro Women," *ibid.* (September, 1903): 434.

ceived in a rural, agricultural America, then should not black American farmers be able to realize it too? The self-sufficient yoeman farmer, not the destitute sharecropper, became the agrarian version of the American Dream. A black farmer who owned his own equipment and land, who had achieved a degree of economic security, and who had a positive sense of himself and his worth became the southern black Horatio Alger.

         ❂   ❂   ❂

How closely did reality mirror or approach the dream? Did the *Southern Workman*'s picture of upward mobility, based upon individual hard work, describe a growing reality? Was the life of black southerners steadily improving during the first thirty years of this century? Unfortunately, the answer to these questions is an emphatic no. If anything, the statistics on landowning and homeowning suggest that black farmers were weakening their position, not improving it. Whereas in 1910, according to one yardstick of progress, there were 220,000 black landowners in the South, by 1930 there were only 183,000. It must be remembered, of course, that the black population, due to migration, decreased during this period.[17] But the glaring fact remains that nearly eighty percent of black farm workers were on the lowest rungs of the economic ladder; they were tenants, sharecroppers, and wage laborers. Even at the close of this period, the overwhelming majority of blacks still lived in the South and their economic condition had not improved.

> Cotton, cotton,
> All we know;
> Plant cotton, hoe it,
> Baig it to grow;
> What good it do to us
> Gawd only know![18]

The reality of life for most black southerners was grim. The future on earth did not contain any hope. The words of the poor, simple black farmer effectively captured his limited horizon:

---

[17] Eighty-nine percent of the black population lived in the South in 1910 while only seventy-eight percent lived there in 1930.

[18] Sterling Brown, "Old King Cotton," in *Southern Road* (New York: Harcourt, Brace, 1932), frontispiece.

> Trouble comes, trouble goes.
> I done had my share of woes.
> Times get better by 'n' by,
> But then my time will come to die.[19]

The next world, rather than this one, offered hope. As one study of religion and the church in the South suggested, otherworldliness dominated the sermons and thoughts of poor blacks.[20] How could it be otherwise? The possibilities of improvement seemed remote and unreal. The soil did not get any better, the white owners did not grow kinder, and the weather continued to be unpredictable. Indeed, heaven became not only the pleasant stuff from which day dreams were made, but also the single hopeful vision in an otherwise clouded picture.

Examples existed, of course, of poor black boys emerging from the impoverished soil of the land to succeed despite all odds. And they wrote down their stories to provide inspiration to the masses who still hoped. William Pickens, the field secretary of the National Association for the Advancement of Colored People in the twenties, described in his autobiography how his father, a farmer laborer, moved from job to job, forever looking for a better way of life. Yet every year he seemed to owe more money to the white master than he had the previous year. "And who could deny it? The white man did all the reckoning." Pickens's mother died when he was thirteen, thereby robbing him of his major support for education and improvement. Pickens commented that "one of the chief causes of the rapid advancement of the Negro race since the Civil War has been the ambition of emancipated black mothers for the education of their children."[21] But, undaunted, this incredibly well motivated and bright young man literally pulled himself out of the southern mire by his bootstraps. His description of how he worked part-time in order to pay for his schooling and how he persevered despite tremendous hardships rivals Ben Franklin's version of the self-made man story.

Pickens, however, was the exception and not the rule. Surely he

[19] Charles S. Johnson, *Shadow of the Plantation* (Chicago: University of Chicago Press, 1934), p. 128.

[20] Benjamin E. Mays and Joseph W. Nicholson, *The Negro's Church* (New York: Institute of Social and Religious Research, 1933), p. 59.

[21] William Pickens, *Bursting Bonds* (Boston: Jordan and Moore Press, 1929), p. 17.

was a living example of someone who overcame the deprivation of being born black in South Carolina to poor, uneducated people. A Yale graduate, valedictorian of his Little Rock, Arkansas, high school class, dean of Morgan College, and then field secretary of the NAACP signify impressive accomplishments. But the overwhelming majority of black peoples' lives could more effectively be summed up as:

> A nought's a nought, and a figger's a figger—
> All fer de white man—none fer de nigger![22]

The daily diet of ninety percent of the black farmers in the South consisted of corn or flour bread and syrup or sorghum. Their one- or two-room cabins were shacks. "My house," said one woman, "is so rotten you kin jest take up the boards in your hand and crumple 'em up. Everything done swunk about it."[23] Barely ten percent of the black residents in Macon County, Alabama, in the late twenties owned their dilapidated houses.[24] Dirt streets and dirt sidewalks characterized the pathways of black America. A barter economy existed for many poor blacks. Money, the basic unit of a capitalistic society, was not used. The black sharecropper exchanged his cotton crop for food and clothes in the white man's store. "You can't do nothing with white folks agin you," commented a black farmer in Alabama.[25] Similarly, you could barely do anything even with white folks for you. The boundaries of action were extremely limited. How much you owed the white owner after working the land for a year was determined by the white man's ledger. How much credit, if any, you would obtain was decided by the white man. *If* you could work the land was also decided by him. Convict leasing, a clever southern device invented to produce free labor, completed this grim scenario. It was no accident that blacks were apprehended in great numbers, dominated the chain gangs, and were leased to white industrialists to build their roads, work their mines, and toil in their factories. The southern states did not have to maintain prisons; white businessmen did not have to employ union workers. Every-

---

[22] *Ibid.*, p. 26.
[23] Johnson, *op. cit.*, p. 99.
[24] *Ibid.*, p. 61.
[25] *Ibid.*, p. 27.

one was happy except for the poor blacks who served in this twen-tieth-century version of slavery.

Thus, reality belied the *Southern Workman*'s portrait of life in the South. Interestingly enough, however, sociological treaties, an-other respectable indicator of the real world, did little to destroy the *Southern Workman*'s image of reality. Black sociologists such as Charles S. Johnson and E. Franklin Frazier interviewed hundreds of black farmers in the South, categorized them into innumerable slots, and concluded that black southerners constituted a peasant class that suffered from isolation and cultural lag. Johnson, who was the National Urban League's editor of *Opportunity* during the early twenties and then head of the social science department at Fisk University in Nashville, studied black southerners within the sociological frame of reference. Although his studies mixed anec-dotal material with statistics and graphs, the objective study, or rather the effort at viewing the reality at a distance, ignored the potent role that white institutional bigotry played in creating black poverty.

No word is said in *Shadow of the Plantation*, based upon 612 families in Macon County, Alabama, of political disfranchisement, unequal educational facilities, job discrimination, or institutional prejudice. Like anthropologists observing an exotic culture (indeed Robert Park's introduction to the volume compares the black folk culture in the South to Redfield's study of Mexican peasants), John-son dispassionately described the multiple family arrangements, the value system, the religious outlook, and so on of his subjects. He laboriously categorized families into groups with typically socio-logical labels such as: "families with strong maternal dominance and with specific moral codes"; "quasi-families: female heads of assembled families"; and "quasi-families: male heads of transient families with shifting family members."[26] In so doing, despite the personal interviews interspersed with the charts and graphs, the human element disappeared and cold, objective numbers remained. Sociology may have been in its golden period, as one recent sociolo-gist has suggested,[27] during the first thirty years of this century, and black sociologists may have shared in its glory, but the evils of the

---

[26] *Ibid.*, pp. 35–9.
[27] Nathan Glazer, introduction to *The Negro Family in the United States*, by E. Franklin Frazier, rev. ed. (Chicago: University of Chicago Press, 1967).

discipline became incredibly glaring when applied to an analysis of the black southerner's life. The accusation that human beings were replaced with statistics has already been leveled.

Another charge, more apt for our discussion of the southern reality in terms of the American Dream, is that black and white sociologists judged the black culture by middle-class white American standards precisely when white middle-class society did not admit eager black members into its midst. The criticism here, it seems to me, is not against the ideals of the American Dream (that is an entirely separate issue), which *is* largely a middle-class dream, but rather against the blindness of supposedly expert observers who ignored the fact that the reality did not allow for the fulfillment of the rhetoric. Southern whites did not provide adequate schooling for blacks. (E. Franklin Frazier noted in one of his studies that "... education is the chief means by which the Negro escapes from the masses into the middle class...."[28]) Black sociologists understandably accepted the American Dream value system. By its standards they had succeeded. By its precepts they had obtained their success.

While cultural lag and isolation explained, according to Charles Johnson, the backwardness of rural black farmers in Macon County, Frazier viewed the black family unit as the crucial determinant of social change. Although he acknowledged the importance of economic opportunity and participation in the life of the community, he concluded that:

> The gains in civilization which result from participation in the white world will in the future as in the past be transmitted to future generations through the family.[29]

The Negro family, as described in both Johnson's and Frazier's study, did not follow middle-class standards. Illegitimacy, according to white Anglo-Saxon norms, was high; marriage and divorce was casual; and the extended rather than the nuclear family predominated. Parental fidelity and stability was deemed crucial to success within the white American scheme. The overall picture presented by the professional sociologists was one of gradual assimilation and

---

[28] *Ibid.*, p. 331.
[29] Frazier, *op. cit.*, p. 368.

acculturation; as black southerners, through education, learned middle-class values and skills, they would eventually work their way out of the peasant mentality and class in which they lived and suffered.

Perpetual poverty, built in inferiority, and the inability to change the environment did not enter into the black sociologist's frame of reference. Their world was a progressive one; their quantitative methods supported the commitment to positive advancement; and the desolate life situation of black farmers in Issaquena County, Mississippi, or Macon County, Alabama, appeared to be a vanishing phenomenon. Rather than depicting the unchanging reality of life for the majority of black southerners, the sociologists thought they were capturing a disappearing culture, a minority remnant of a folk tradition. The fact that black Americans were still largely rural and southern in 1930, and not urban and northern, did not impress itself fully on their minds. The North, migration, and the big cities characterized the wave of the future. To the poor southern blacks, there was no consolation in this judgment. Life went inexorably and miserably on as it had in previous years.

Private property, especially the private owning of land, constituted the backbone of the American Dream and most especially the southern American system. The *Southern Workman,* a product after all of southern culture, accepted this value. It inhered in all of its statements. If the black sharecropper worked hard, saved his money (an unreality in a barter economy), and was respectful to the white powers, then he could gain his modest portion of the dream. Further, the black Christian distrust of the city, similar to the fundamentalist white Protestant's, confirmed the belief that the southern rural way of life, with its emphasis upon personalism, family loyalty, and stability were virtues that would be lost elsewhere. Thus, the church supported the status quo and encouraged the yeoman farmer virtues.

All of these factors, combined with the southern antagonism toward collectivity, became the potent tools to keep southern blacks in their places in the South. Any effort of blacks to organize was ruthlessly suppressed. Moreover, the southern white value system viewed success, power, and achievement from an individualistic perspective, and rhetorically stood for each person's power to determine, shape, and effect his own destiny. This example merely illustrates hypocrisy on the part of southern whites; but their unwillingness to tax themselves is partially, at least, based upon the conviction that individuals and families should take care of themselves, not the collective state. Poverty, of course, also contributed to the economic impossibility to raise taxes and provide services to the community. Poor whites and poor blacks (and the number of poor whites in the South was enormous) shared a dismal way of life. A southern white sharecropper and a black sharecropper lived the same kind of life of quiet desperation. Neither group acted as a group because of their basic acceptance of their own impotence. The *Southern Workman* encouraged collective effort in agricultural matters; that is, the sharing of farming knowledge and equipment, but they never extended the principle. They never entertained the radical notion of collective farms, of collective purchasing and selling, or of collective bargaining with the white master.

In ideology and theology, poor black southerners shared the poor white southerners' fear of organization as un-American, as a betrayal somehow of the essence of democracy. Of course they also feared the realistic terror and violence that would result from any effort toward collectivity. It is hard, if not impossible, to determine from the inarticulate majority which of these beliefs played a predominant role, or which was the most influential. The only words of black farmers that we hear have been captured in print as anecdotes in the notes of a sociologist, or in black newspaper accounts in Chicago. They depict, in grim, specific detail, the horrid life lived by black Mississippians and Alabamans but they do not discuss in abstract, intellectual terms their attitudes or beliefs. They reflect a real understanding of the power of the white man and their corresponding powerlessness. They express a tremendous feeling of paralysis and helplessness. Perhaps the North, in the years 1900–1930, offered the safety valve for the aggressive discontents, those who did not, and could not, resign themselves to the degrading reality. The North became, to courageous and adamant black southerners, what the West was to ambitious and unhappy whites in the nineteenth century. And the American Dream presented itself in an urban environment to the arriving black immigrant from the farm.

Chapter 3

The Urban View of the Dream

An articulate, productive, urban black intellectual elite existed in this country by 1900. They wrote frequent articles for both white and black magazines, mainly urban based, and they demonstrated a complete commitment to the American Dream. Black writers accepted the values of white America. They agreed that education was the key to mobility; that mobility, indeed, could be achieved by hard working, disciplined blacks; and that the evidence suggested a bright and progressive future for black people in America. Kelly Miller, for example, a prominent black sociologist at Howard University and one of the leading black thinkers of the period, frequently wrote articles that exemplified his faith in the American Dream. In "The Negro's Part in the Negro Problem," Miller contended that the present evils of black life in the North—criminality, illiteracy, and unemployment—could easily be eradicated if the white man allowed blacks to be properly educated, clothed, and housed.[1] The backwardness of the black race, Miller argued, was environmentally determined and therefore changeable. Opportunity, the chief necessity, would eliminate all social ills. How this

---

[1] Kelly Miller, "The Negro's Part in the Negro Problem," *Forum* 36 (October, 1904): 289–304.

opportunity was to be obtained from a recalcitrant white majority was not explained. As in much of the writing of the period, the specific methodology was not described. Intellectuals, then and now, often view their major task as articulation of problems and not as providing the concrete steps to their solution.

In a piece written near the end of the 1920s, Miller discussed the black problem in somewhat different terms. First, he distinguished between the goal of equality and the goal of equal opportunity and argued that the latter, rather than the former, should be the black man's ideal. However, after emancipation, many black men mistakenly expected to achieve complete equality. Miller went on to state that blacks have distinctive traits and should not want to imitate whites. They could teach white Americans their special music, their style of living, and their adaptability. The goal of the black American, he further argued, should be equal opportunity to achieve the material benefits of the society but to preserve and assert the cultural uniqueness of black men.[2] During the twenties, this theme became the dominant one: economic, political, and educational fulfillment within the American framework coupled with the essential need for cultural autonomy. These two goals, moreover, were seen as harmonious and interwoven.

The majority of the articles on the black American dealt with specific components of the race problem; that is, most writers focused upon black education, politics, or economics in their discussions. They implicitly accepted the view that the structures of American society were valid and that each factor within it could effectuate desirable change. Thus, a writer dealing with education accepted all of the American assumptions about education and its powerful role in American life. He accepted, without ever stating it, his belief that by improving, adding, changing, or aiding the educational factor, the black American's life would be materially benefited. From the point of view of many black writers, education was *the* means of developing black leadership. W. E. B. DuBois, a professor and writer with impressive academic credentials and one of the leading black spokesmen in the first thirty years of this century, advocated identifying and educating the talented one-tenth of the black population. In contrast with him, Booker T. Washington, con-

---

[2] Kelly Miller, "What Has the Negro to Give?," *Christian Century,* 4 August, 1927, pp. 921–23.

sidered by white America to be the spokesman for black America, emphasized vocational education for the black masses, and was less interested in producing black Ph.D.'s. But the significant point here is the commitment to education as the mobilizing and equalizing factor in American society.

Alain Locke, a major contributor to the Harlem Renaissance in the twenties, also wrote about black education.[3] He criticized the paternalistic and conservative nature of the black colleges and urged the development of a vigorous black leadership. He also wanted to see black schools become autonomous. Simultaneous with this desire, however, Locke advocated interracial schools as he considered separatist schools bad for both races. Thus, he anticipated one of the crucial problems facing blacks and whites in America. If the two races are educated separately, live apart from each other, and work in distinctly different types of jobs, there will never be biracial equality and harmony. In the twenties, most of the major black spokesmen vigorously supported integrated schools, but they found little support for this view. Further, they handled the seeming contradiction between advocating integrated education *and* urging black control of black colleges by pragmatically pointing out the fact that ninety percent of black college students were in segregated schools and they had to be given a better education. Thus, Locke could note the injustice and undemocratic nature of segregated schools, but still address the bulk of his remarks to the need for more vigorous black leadership in the black schools.

Alain Locke wanted black colleges to produce socially conscious black men who would work for the betterment of the race. In the twenties, there was a conspicuous lack of interest on the part of many college educated black men to participate in reform activities. Locke blamed the colleges for this lack of social commitment. All black leaders appreciated the fact that a literate, skilled population was essential to the progress of the race. During the twenties, black students at black schools such as Fisk University in Nashville, Tennessee, and Howard University in Washington, D. C., demanded changes in their curriculum and administration. White presidents of black schools, a typical pattern, were challenged for the first time. Mordecai Wyatt Johnson became the first black president of

---

[3] Alain Locke, "Negro Education Bids for Par," *Survey*, 1 September 1925, pp. 567–70, 592–93.

Howard University while the white president of Fisk called in the police in February, 1925, to break up a student strike. After he had a number of students arrested, a large portion of the student body went home in protest; the president was forced to resign. Although another white man replaced him, one black man described the new president as "the blackest white man I have ever known."[4] More blacks were going to college and more were demanding an upgrading in their education. Black students proudly asserted their desire for autonomy and local control of their institutions. They also wanted to see less paternalizing and less missionizing in their schools. They did not articulate, however, the social consciousness desired by Alain Locke.

Perhaps the most typical *white* view of the role of education for black men was given by the editors of the *Outlook,* a rather conservative magazine of the period. In an editorial entitled "Shall the Negro Be Educated?" they answered their question in the pragmatic terms for which Americans are well known. After rejecting two other solutions to the Negro problem—exportation and intermingling—they concluded that the only alternative was to educate black men or ". . . to leave them to increasing degeneration and decay, a burden and a peril alike to themselves and to their neighbors."[5] In a sense they posed an evolutionary argument in reverse: if blacks were not educated, they would regress and return to an earlier stage of human development. "Left uneducated," the editors warned their readers, "to drop in successive generations into ever lower stages of barbarism, they will be a burden bound upon the back of the South, if not a millstone bound about its neck."[6] Thus, the education of the black man became a practical solution to a very bad problem indeed. It was the lesser of evils and the only possible way of making blacks self-sufficient; the editor hastened to add that "manual and industrial training" should be the direction that black education should take. Apparently, in the editor's mind, evolutionary change for black men was only possible in one direction—backwards.

In quickly rejecting the other solutions to the problem, the *Outlook* editors repudiated the two radical ways of dealing with the

---

[4] John R. Scotford, "The New Negro Education," *Christian Century,* 12 January 1928, p. 48.

[5] Editorial, "Shall the Negro Be Educated?," *Outlook,* 4 May 1901, p. 13.

[6] *Ibid.*

black problem in America. They accepted, for all intents and purposes, the need to deal with black Americans within the geographic as well as intellectual boundaries of America. Yet they viewed intermarriage on a wide scale and the eventual elimination of the color line as clearly outside the realm of desirability. The theme of social equality, one which we will turn to later, was not even bridged. Education must be provided for black men, but limited education with limited goals. This "solution" demonstrated one of the dilemmas of this complex problem. White America raised the sights of black Americans by educating them but then blocked their vision. Some education, yes, but not with a view toward equality, mobility, or abundance. A little of the American Dream, but not all of it. A diluted form but not the authentic, complete form. While black writers discussed whether classical or vocational education would most effectively help black Americans, and debated their hierarchy of priorities, white Americans had already decided what kind of education black Americans would have.

The gap between the white and black attitudes toward education for blacks cannot be overstressed. Black and white writers, both products of the American system and generally committed to it, assumed the validity and necessity of education for all Americans. But the nature and extent of that education differed dramatically. White writers predetermined the restrictive nature of black education while black writers debated the proper kind of education for the second generation removed from slavery. While Booker T. Washington, a very pragmatic American, viewed economic self-sufficiency as the basic goal for the mass of black Americans, W. E. B. DuBois considered trained and talented black leaders as the major necessity.

Obviously, the kind of education provided for blacks would be determined by the prevailing educational philosophy. The southern bent of Washington's view,[7] developed in a rural, agricultural world that he knew so well, was in stark contrast to the northern quality of DuBois's view. To the well-educated mulatto from Massachusetts, the urban-industrial scene became the major focal point for

---

[7] Washington was born a slave and raised in the South; he was a graduate of Hampton Institute and the founder of Tuskegee Institute in Alabama, a school committed to the same goals as Hampton. DuBois was born and raised in Massachusetts, received a Ph.D. from Harvard, and was a sociology professor at Atlanta University before he came to New York and became the editorial director of the newly formed NAACP in 1910.

black life and advancement. Thus, DuBois's educational philosophy, molded in a different setting of the American Dream, would naturally see the accomplishment of the dream for black Americans in a way that the agrarian environment of Washington would not. Both geographic, economic, and cultural landscapes, however, were American and both provided authentic interpretations of how the dream could be realized for black Americans. The kind of education, whether it be to achieve self-sufficient farmers or an urban intelligensia, would result in genuine American types. Alain Locke appreciated the contribution of Booker T. Washington and, from the perspective of the mid-twenties, saw the Hampton-Tuskegee model as supplementary to the liberal arts college. The feuding between them was diminishing, he gladly reported, and both kinds of schools provided necessary educational opportunities for black Americans.[8]

In turning from education, a very American goal, to politics, we are also turning to a very American feature of our culture. Political power is based upon the holiest of American principles: participatory democracy. Voting, attending political meetings, expressing opinions in political discussions, and being involved in the selection of political representatives are some of the most vital traditions in American democracy. Thus, when northern black writers in the early years of this century discussed political consciousness as a goal of black Americans, they were operating within the American framework of desired ideals.

The discussion of politics in northern urban magazines, in contrast to its omission from the pages of the *Southern Workman*, demonstrated the writers' belief that political democracy was feasible in the North. *Crisis*, the organ of the NAACP with headquarters in New York, became a leading advocate of political equality for black Americans. W. E. B. DuBois edited the journal and frequently described the black man's role, or potential role, in politics. The white intellectual supporters of the NAACP, most notably Mary White Ovington, Moorfield Storey, and Oswald Garrison Villard, also contributed articles on this subject.

The methods utilized to call black Americans' attention to the political situation in America were typically American. DuBois wrote articles describing the problem and offered solutions to it.

---

[8] Locke, *op. cit.*

The NAACP initiated law suits in the courts to stop legal disfranchisement. The NAACP leaders argued that the spirit and the letter of the Fourteenth and Fifteenth Amendments to the Constitution had been violated, and the courts had to grant black Americans the same basic citizenship rights as all other Americans. Thus, legal and informational weapons were used by the NAACP and *Crisis* to bring the story of political inequality home to blacks and whites. The courts and the magazine became the chief arenas for discussion of political equality, two institutions that have been specifically designed to protect and acquaint Americans with their basic rights.

W. E. B. DuBois was the major spokesman for political rights for black America both in the pages of *Crisis* and the popular magazines. DuBois's main political advice during this period was for black men, particularly in communities such as New York's Harlem, to choose their political representatives carefully, depending upon their promises and actions for black Americans. His advice was pragmatic and realistic. Do not follow any party blindly. Knowing of the southern blacks' dutiful obedience to the Republican party in the South, DuBois counselled discreet selection of the best political candidate for black men, regardless of party label. And if neither party offered good choices, then he suggested that the blacks put up their own candidate and support him completely.[9] Using the example of the Woman's party in 1916, DuBois editorialized that block voting was essential to success. Every interest group, he reasoned, should vote together. Just as women had to stay together to be a meaningful political power, so blacks had to do the same thing.

Although DuBois found the national Democratic party wanting, the Republicans provided no alternative. His choice for president in 1912 was Woodrow Wilson, but it was a reluctant choice based upon practical necessity. His ideal choice was Eugene Debs; but being politically astute, DuBois advised his readers not to vote for the Socialist candidate. DuBois's disappointment with Wilson became an enduring theme during the Wilson years in office especially with the prominence of Southern Democrats in Washington during his tenure. In the Republican twenties, DuBois contented himself with supporting local Democrats, most notably Harlem Democrats,

---

[9] W. E. DuBois, "The Negro Party," *Crisis* 12 (October, 1916): 268. See also DuBois's "The Republicans and the Black Voter," *Nation*, 5 June 1920, pp. 757–58; and "Is Al Smith Afraid of the South?," *ibid.*, 17 October 1928, pp. 392–94, for some examples of his political views.

who spoke to the needs of black people. In 1928, he hoped that Al Smith would boldly take a stand on civil rights and break the stranglehold that the South had on the Democratic party.[10] American democracy was on trial, DuBois argued, and the Democratic presidential candidate was obligated to act positively for the rights of black Americans.

Political success, of course, was not achieved during this period; blacks who voted in the urban areas of the North often found themselves absorbed into the Republican party machine. In the South, the blacks simply could not vote. The only national black politician to be elected to office during the first thirty years of this century was Oscar De Priest, who in 1928 became the first black member of the House of Representatives since Reconstruction. His election to office, coming from the First Congressional District of Illinois, depended upon the support of the Republican machine in Chicago; De Priest obviously could not, singlehandedly, pass legislation that would be favorable to black Americans. But the goal and the rhetorical appeal to political ideals continued, despite the poor results. The myth of political democracy and the weight placed upon political participation have continued to endure, despite the statistics indicating political apathy and the extreme lack of participation in politics—even by the white majority that can readily exercise the franchise.

Many cynics, as well as statisticians, have observed that the foundation of American democracy is based precisely upon the fact that there is minimal participation in politics. A sorry thought, no doubt, and one which black intellectuals in the first third of this century decried. Democracy and participation were intertwined and crucial to the success of the American system. DuBois frequently phrased his political discussions in terms of American democracy being on trial—with poor voter turnouts being symptomatic of the demise of democracy. DuBois, I am sure, would have scoffed at the satirical view that apathy was the very strength of American democracy.

Just as education and politics are significant ingredients in the building of American citizens (and in achieving the American Dream) so, too, is economics a core issue. Black writers frequently concerned themselves with the economic progress of blacks. While

---

[10] DuBois, "Is Al Smith Afraid of the South?," *op. cit.*

the *Southern Workman* devoted numerous articles to the economic training programs available for black farmers and often described the economic success of black businessmen, *Crisis* provided both northern and southern examples of black capitalism. Developing a black middle class, composed of skilled black workers, professionals, and white collar workers, was the aim of all black leaders. *Crisis* often reported on the economic accomplishments of black men to serve as inspirations to their black brothers. In this way, they shared with the *Southern Workman* the function of propagandizing for the American Dream; they confirmed its reality by offering examples of individual successes. Every example of economic progress, agricultural and urban, was enthusiastically noted. "A. H. Holmes, a prominent Negro farmer, has grown two acres of rice in McRae, Georgia, in a region where it was not thought hitherto that rice could be raised."[11] Tidbits such as this frequently sprinkled the pages of the *Crisis* to support the general view that real progress was being made and that the black man was rapidly becoming a self-sufficient, autonomous economic asset to his community.

The formation of the National Negro Business League in 1900 by Booker T. Washington heralded the cooperative efforts of black men to meet and discuss common business problems. Robert Moton, who succeeded Washington at Tuskegee Institute in Alabama in 1915, frequently spoke about the merits and accomplishments of the league. Statistics describing the capital assets of individual black men, the amount of property owned, and the number of enterprises in which black men were engaged dotted every issue of *Crisis*. All of the black leaders, in fact, indulged in statistical discussions in an effort to prove, to themselves and their white and black audiences, that substantive progress had been made by black men in a very short period of time. Simultaneous with their announcements of progress, however, were their reminders to their audiences of the great amount of work yet to be done. Clearly, black entrepreneurs were an infinitesimal portion of the black population in America. However great the accomplishments, and they were surely significant given the disadvantages under which they operated and their recent starting point, they did not describe the economic position of the overwhelming majority of black Americans.

But economic mobility is a crucial factor in the American Dream

---

[11] News item, *Crisis* 5 (November, 1912): 7.

mythology. Evidence of it sustains the believers and the articulators of the dream. It also propels people into behaving and conforming to the outlines of the myth. Thus, the *Southern Workman* and *Crisis* constantly reminded their readers of the possibilities of economic success if only they devoted themselves diligently to their work, practiced the Protestant virtues of thrift and hard work, and patiently persevered.[12] *Opportunity*, the journal of the Urban League, often dealt with the specific urban labor problems that blacks faced in the cities of the North. With the new tools of sociology as their weapon, the Urban League, a sister organization of the NAACP, gathered statistical evidence, conducted investigations on urban working conditions, and generally reported the economic progress being made by blacks. One of the key problems with which they had to deal was that of the black worker, who competed with white workers for a limited number of jobs. Ever since blacks began moving into northern cities, they had been used as strikebreakers. Many a strike in Chicago, Philadelphia, and New York had been broken with the aid of black workers.

Black intellectuals deplored the use of black labor as scabs and tried to eliminate it. They urged the unions to admit black men on an equal basis with whites and to eliminate the color struggle for jobs. Richard R. Wright, Jr., a black minister and sociologist, argued as early as 1905 that black workers were not willing to act as strikebreakers and that, given an opportunity, they would become loyal union workers who could, and would, perform their jobs diligently. Using examples from three Chicago strikes, the building trades in 1900, the teamsters in 1905, and the meatpackers in 1904, Wright said that blacks did not become strikebreakers and that the unions promised them entry.[13] Obviously, the unions would attempt to lure blacks away from their activity as strikebreakers until the danger of a strike was over. Did they then fulfill their promises and accept the black workers into their unions on an equal basis? Unfortunately, the evidence does not suggest that the majority of unions lived up to their pledges.

Yet, black leaders always coupled their discussions of limited

---

[12] See, for example, Albon L. Holsey, "Meeting Chain Store Competition Through Cooperation," *Southern Workman* 58 (July, 1929): 298–301.

[13] R. R. Wright, Jr., "The Negro in Times of Industrial Unrest," *Charities*, 17 October 1905, pp. 69–73.

economic success with the abstract hope that economic progress was inevitable. Perhaps it is the belief in the inevitability of progress that provided the certainty and perseverance that infused the writings of black spokesmen. Eugene Kinckle Jones, for example, the executive secretary of the Urban League in the twenties, continuously symbolized and expressed the commitment to progress for blacks. In one speech he gave in Canton, Ohio, and reprinted in *Opportunity* (indeed the very title of the magazine is the essence of the American Dream!), Jones reasoned that economic competition is the core of modern life. "Success in life calls for thorough preparation. Success in American life today is fraught with keen competition."[14] Jones pointed to the fact that there were six hundred black public school teachers in New York City in 1928 to symbolize the dramatic success of black New Yorkers. The beginnings of a significant professional class were evident, according to Jones, and the success of the six hundred could be multiplied infinitely if blacks appreciated the need for "thorough preparation."

Indeed, the inevitability of progress pervaded most discussions of economics, politics, and education. Jones's remarks are very typical in this respect. In the speech just referred to, he traced the 250-year history of the American Negro and concluded that it was a "golden age" despite "a series of unjust and discouraging events which would have spelled disaster to any less hopeful race of people. . . ." He then went on to list the lynchings, peonage, segregation laws, and general denial of rights as examples of the negative events which marred the black man's experience in America. But he insisted that the facts only "tended to arrest the upward curve making his [Negro's] progress."

We could show without question various lines of group improvement in Negro life in America which would demonstrate beyond doubt that here in our native land is the most hopeful spot on the globe for a favorable social improvement experiment for the Negro which may serve as a model for Negro groups elsewhere in the world. The white race and the Negro race in America are each possessed of heritages and have had racial experience so vastly different. They are given an unusual opportunity to prove

---

[14] Eugene K. Jones, "The Negro's Opportunity Today," *Opportunity* 6 (January, 1928): 11.

the possibilities of a true democracy where different races of mankind may live in peace and harmony, each one giving of his best to the welfare of all and to the glory of God and man.[15]

This lengthy quotation effectively captures the hopeful tone and the persistent theme of the period. The overwhelming number of magazine articles written during the first thirty years of this century reflected this faith and hope in American democracy.

Thus, black commentary on economics remained in the American mold; even when socialist DuBois discussed economics, and the need for cooperatives among black businessmen, he remained within the American framework. DuBois stressed the need for black men to buy and own property in Harlem; to start black businesses so that blacks did not have to patronize white stores; and to build, quite consciously, a black bourgeoisie that was socially responsible to its black proletarian brothers. All of these economic goals, however, are very American goals too. This kind of economic program is domesticated socialism. Private property, acquired through legal channels, may be turned into socialist property but in no way are the virtues of the sanctity of property and the power of capital denied. Most black writers and thinkers recognized the power of wealth and preached implementing the American goals of economic success. They did not repudiate the traditional methods of accumulating wealth; neither did they suggest revolution as the necessary precondition to the attainment of their utopia.[16]

The issue of social equality was surely the most heated and emotional of all the components of the American Dream. Educational, political, and economic opportunity and equality can be discussed dispassionately by its advocates and critics. However, no such temper could characterize discussions of social equality. To the white southerner, of course, this was the hard core of the matter. The desire for social equality was the basis for all of the black man's civil rights goals. Or to put it another way, the prevention of social equality, to a racist, was the foundation upon which one built discrimination in every other area of life. Equality in politics, economics, and education would ultimately lead blacks into your parlor. Blacks would get uppity ideas if they could vote, go to school,

---

[15] *Ibid.*
[16] See Chapter 5 for a further discussion of this topic.

and improve their economic position. They would want to talk on an equal basis with white folks and try to be *just like them.*

Southerners were always more candid on this point than northerners. They knew that equal treatment meant precisely that. To prevent any blacks from raising their hopes, white southerners simply denied the whole American Dream to blacks. Economic self-sufficiency, in its place, as advocated by the *Southern Workman,* was acceptable, but only within the limited sphere of the black community. Blacks could improve themselves within black society but they could never hope to cross the line into white society. The Declaration of Independence and the Constitution never meant, according to the southern view, that blacks were inherently equal or that the American ideas were written for them. In this sense, the white southerners were more consistent and honest in their race relations. They never believed that the American Dream included the blacks; therefore, they never articulated the rhetoric when dealing with blacks and they never conceded equality in any sphere of life.

In the North, where the rhetoric was often used more freely, the problem of social equality had to be faced. DuBois spoke to this issue frequently, as did other black leaders.[17] In many discussions for *Crisis,* DuBois expressed his views on the subject of intermarriage.[18] White attitudes toward intermarriage touched the core of their racial beliefs. Discussions of political, economic, or educational equality were only surface considerations of the real issue, namely, whether blacks and whites would interact on every possible level with one another and whether they would talk to each other, socialize, and possibly mate.

It is the most frightful indictment of a country which dares to call itself civilized that it has allowed itself to drift into a state of ignorance where ten million people are coming to believe that

---

[17] Radical black leaders such as A. Philip Randolph and Monroe Trotter often insisted upon the right of social equality too. They, however, never expressed themselves on this subject in the popular magazines of the day. Rather, they both wrote for their respective journals which reached very few people.

[18] See especially the following articles by DuBois from *Crisis:* "Work for Black Folk in 1914," February, 1914; "The Immediate Program of the American Negro," April, 1915; "The Social Equality of Whites and Blacks," November, 1920; and "Intermarriage," April, 1925.

all white people are liars and thieves, and the whites in turn to believe that the chief industry of Negroes is raping white women.

Because the two races have infrequent contacts with one another, a whole set of distorted views and stereotypes have developed. Further, DuBois believed, as every true humanist did, that social equality was a human right to which every human being was entitled. Although he did not believe that it was expedient in 1920 for blacks and whites to intermarry, given the climate of opinion in the country, he believed it was each individual's right to do as he chose.[19]

Sexual intimacy was practiced in America as witnessed by the high mulatto population but social equality as a principle was repudiated. If you relinquished the principle, however, DuBois argued that you conceded the argument to racists and acknowledged the differences (and hence inequality) between the races. If God wanted black and white people not to mate, one black writer sardonically pointed out, He would have made them in such a way that it would be biologically impossible for them to do so.[20] Thus, social equality became the substantive issue and the one which tested the validity of the American Dream most effectively. But, as would be expected, most writers did not address themselves to this question but rather chose to interpret the American Dream as only including political, educational, and economic rights and not social rights.

The president of the United States, Warren G. Harding, expressed the prevalent interpretation of the relationship of the dream to black Americans. In a speech in Birmingham, Alabama, on October 25, 1921, Harding asserted the equality of the black man in political and economic matters, but carefully noted that this equality did not apply to social and racial spheres. Separatism, rather than Americanism, would prevail in the delicate areas of life. The speech was reported extensively and quite approvingly. This, then, would be the interpretation of the American Dream in relation to black Americans: equality of opportunity in political and economic matters, but

---

[19] DuBois, "The Immediate Program of the American Negro," *ibid.*, p. 311; and DuBois, "The Social Equality of Whites and Blacks," *ibid.*

[20] Helen M. Chesnutt, *Charles Waddell Chesnutt: Pioneer of the Color Line* (Chapel Hill: University of North Carolina Press, 1952), p. 233.

separation in social and racial affairs. Limited application of the American Dream or, as many articulators of the dream probably argued, the legitimate interpretation of it. After all, what else did America guarantee her citizens other than political participation and economic and educational opportunity? Basic civil rights (basic human rights, according to this view) were not embodied in the American Dream. This point of view added insult to injury from the point of view of black Americans. First, white America hypocritically preached American (political and economic) goals as being attainable but in reality denied them to black citizens. Then, in self-righteous tones, they insisted that the dream only applied to those same areas!

DuBois's response to the Harding speech turned out to be prophetic. If Harding wanted the black people to develop pride and to focus solely upon the accomplishments of their own group and stay together, then the results would portend disaster for all Americans. "For the day," he warned, "that Black men love Black men simply because they are Black, is the day they will hate White men simply because they are White. And then, God help us all!"[21] Social equality, human equality based upon respect for humanness, DuBois said, was essential. Differences between people had to be founded upon differences in ability and accomplishment, not upon any definition of inherent differences. Conversely, sympathy and loyalty had to be established according to principles and actions too, and not color. Racism, black or white, was an unacceptable philosophy for all people. The American Dream had to be founded upon color blindness, otherwise the word American should be amended to read: white American Dream.

But the words and views of DuBois did not influence or change the minds of most white Americans. Implicitly, they accepted President Harding's analysis of the issue. Most black Americans, similarly, seemed to believe, at least in the first third of this century, that the achievement of political, economic, and educational equality—a mighty achievement—would fulfill their hopes. If America provided these accomplishments for her black citizens, she would be generous indeed.

In a sense, this view was bolstered by the Harlem Renaissance.

---

[21] W. E. B. DuBois, "President Harding and Social Equality," *Crisis* 23 (December, 1921): 56.

The outpouring of music, poetry, plays, and novels by black artists in Harlem in the twenties aggressively lauded blackness, separateness, and black cultural autonomy. Black writers advocated preserving the uniqueness of black men; they dissuaded their brothers from assimilating, or wanting to assimilate. Although specific writings on this subject will be dealt with later, it is appropriate at this time to consider some of the remarks, aired in the popular journals, on the subject of culture and black Americans.

The American Dream myth does not, of course, necessitate the complete conformity of any individual or group. But it does assume that, with equal opportunity, all Americans will choose common goals, rewards, and artifacts. Thus, all middle-class Americans will share certain styles of living, material accouterments, and values. People of similar social outlook will vote similarly and live in the same kinds of houses. A certain amount of uniformity is assumed. Respect for difference and the preservation of difference is really not an essential part of the dream myth. Americans tolerate difference; they do not respect it. In fact, the dream is often viewed in very standard terms; the stereotypes that have arisen regarding the life-style of the self-made man, of the success story, are all remarkably alike. The Doris Day–Rock Hudson version of the American Dream is homogenized and sanforized. Variations from the stereotypical way of fulfilling the dream are suspect.

Thus, the Harlem Renaissance's emphasis upon cultural difference can be viewed as antithetical to, or certainly apart from, the dream myth. Some black writers, in fact, who criticized the mystique of blackness in the twenties, did it in terms of the Americanism of the blacks. If black Americans have imbibed the values and culture of America, for good or ill, then they could not possess a separate culture. They accepted the values and the conformity of America; they too rejected difference as much as white Americans did. (The argument of the twenties has begun again in our times and the terms of the argument have not changed substantially.) George S. Schuyler, a black critic, for example, had a lively exchange in the *Nation* with poet Langston Hughes on this subject. Schuyler contended that "aside from his color, which ranges from very dark brown to pink, your American Negro is just plain American."[22] American values have been absorbed by black Americans as well

---

[22] George S. Schuyler, "The Negro-Art Hokum," *Nation*, 16 June 1926, p. 662.

as white Americans. "In the homes of the black and white Americans of the same cultural and economic level," Schuyler continued, "one finds similar furniture, literature, and conversation."[23]

Langston Hughes responded that the whiteness of black artists was a problem. Because white values dominate American society, most middle- and upper-class blacks, including the intellectuals, imitate whites and want to be like white people. But in the lower class, Hughes argued, the individuality and soul of the black man is still apparent. "Why should I want to be white?" Hughes asked, "I am a Negro—and beautiful!"[24] The black man was individual in a standardized America, according to the poet, and he should courageously preserve his individuality. In a sense, this view repudiates the rewards of the American Dream. It questions the results of following the conventional political, educational, and economic avenues of America. It suggests a cultural autonomy based upon different values and goals. However, no serious probing of the implications or possible contradictions between cultural differences and the American way in other areas of life were explored in the periodical literature. The prevailing view seemed to be that both were attainable—cultural separatism *and* political, economic, and educational integration.

Eugene Gordon, a black writer who often commented on the classes within black society, noted in one article that the charge of imitation was meaningless: "Having been schooled in American institutions, there is nothing for either to do but conform. There remains for the black man, as for the white, nothing but to assimilate the American culture and to be assimilated into the general scheme."[25] This cultural determinist view pervaded much of the critical writing about the Harlem Renaissance. Black and white Americans, having been exposed to the same values, therefore shared the same dreams. Gordon sardonically concluded his analysis by saying that progress for blacks meant imitating the whites, adopting their "snobbery and class distinctions and tinsel riches ..."[26] and aspiring to their false gods of materialism and emptiness. The American Dream, with all of its materialistic excesses, is the

---

[23] *Ibid.*, p. 663.

[24] Langston Hughes, "The Negro Artist and the Racial Mountain," *ibid.*, 23 June 1926, p. 694.

[25] Eugene Gordon, "Negro Society," *Scribner's Monthly* 88 (August, 1930): 137.

[26] *Ibid.*, p. 142.

black man's dream too. Whether it is a qualitatively high culture or not, black Americans wanted the tinsel riches too. Harlem Renaissance writers criticized the American Dream myth precisely because of its superficial qualities, its artificial culture, and its demand for uniformity. Their criticism was cultural. But they were the minority. Most black writers, on the other hand, criticized the hypocrisy of whites who articulated the dream but denied black Americans access to it. When most writers in the magazines of the period spoke directly to the subject of American values, they accepted their worth but decried their lack of fulfillment.

In addition to the numerous pragmatic discussions of how black progress could be achieved, black writers also wrote about the horrible gap between the ideal of the dream and reality. The basic documents of America adequately and eloquently describe the principles upon which this country was founded. The American Dream mythology is bound to the views articulated in them. Thus, by joining discussions of race with the Declaration of Independence and the pertinent amendments to the Constitution, blacks asked their readers to examine the meaning of American ideals. From both a moral and psychological point of view, the appeal to American rhetoric indicated that the resolution of the black-white issue inheres in those very documents; in fact, it was the immediate violation of the letter and spirit of those documents that created the problem. In the twentieth century, many black writers argued, the violation had to end and the words had to become relevant and true for all Americans.

The tone of many of these articles was strident and ironic. How could it be otherwise? These writers stressed the positive aspects of American values; they did not repudiate the virtues of hard work, thrift, justice, and accomplishment. They only desired to see these virtues rewarded when practiced by black Americans. Writers, appealing to the American value system, were, after all, in a difficult position. How do you say to your white audience, in a polite and tactful way, "You are a hypocrite"? How do you implore whites to live up to their own words without criticizing them? How do you do this without whining or sounding mawkish? It was not easy. The patience of black writers was often tested and they frequently couched their exasperation in effective, paradoxical terms. For example, Charles S. Johnson, the editor of *Opportunity*, cogently captured the paradox in this remark about the blacks: "They are expected to prove their worth by producing great statesmen when they are not allowed to vote or hold responsible offices."[27] The Chicago *Whip* noted regarding the blacks' participation in World War I: "The black man fought to make the world safe for democracy; he now demands that America be made safe for black Americans."[28]

When one southern white man suggested that the new black militancy that erupted after the First World War was initiated by German subversion, James Weldon Johnson, the field secretary of the NAACP, could barely contain his reply. Since his organization had been included in the man's indictment, Johnson felt compelled to remind whites that the goals of the NAACP as well as the goals of black Americans were not radical. All they wanted was the fulfillment

> . . . of the guarantees in the Constitution, for the impartial interpretation and application of the law, and for common justice and equal opportunities for the Negro. If this is radicalism, God save the Negro from his conservative friends![29]

The dignified Archibald Grimké reminded the readers of the prestigious *Atlantic Monthly* that the Negro

> knows that his freedom, his American citizenship, his right to vote, have been written into the Constitution of the United States, and written there in three great amendments. He knows more: he knows that he himself has written his title to those rights with his blood in the history of the country in four wars, and he is of the firm belief that his title to them is a perfect one.[30]

The black man's participation in American wars, most especially, the First World War, the war to make the world safe for democracy,

---

[27] Charles S. Johnson, "Some Handicaps of the Negro," *Missionary Review of the World* 49 (June, 1926): 44.

[28] Rollin Lynde Hartt, "The New Negro," *Independent*, 15 January 1921, p. 60.

[29] James Weldon Johnson, "The Negro in War-Time," *Public*, 21 September 1918, p. 1219.

[30] Archibald Grimké, "Why Disfranchisement Is Bad," *Atlantic* 94 (July, 1904): 73.

was frequently recalled to point up the terrible irony. The Negro soldier, according to another writer, was the "embodiment of the joint guardianship of and participation in that abstract democracy for which the Negro was giving his life and buying bonds."[31] The rhetorical question was asked again and again: How could America ask some of her citizens to sacrifice their lives for their country when America did not protect those same citizens' basic rights?

"This society exists," exclaimed the *Nation* publisher, Oswald Garrison Villard, "in order to combat the spirit of persecution and prejudice which confronts the colored people of this land,

> and to assure to them every right, privilege and opportunity to which every citizen of the United States is entitled. That it exists at all is in itself an indictment of our American democracy.[32]

Herbert Seligmann asked: "What place is there in a democracy for permanently distinct racial groups who accept that democracy on its own terms?"[33] And in another context, he said,

> There is no race question independent of other problems of democracy; race relations constitute democracy's most essential problem, a problem compounded of all the other adjustments which free men are called upon to make in forming and maintaining social relations.[34]

Walter White, a writer and staff member of the NAACP, in discussing the difficulties of Detroit's black population in obtaining adequate housing wryly noted: "American democracy would be a poor thing indeed if such a desire for better conditions did not develop."[35]

Alain Locke expressed the same concerns but in a different way.

---

[31] Herbert J. Seligmann, "Democracy and Jim-Crowism," *New Republic*, 3 September 1919, p. 151.

[32] Oswald Garrison Villard, "The Objects of the NAACP," *Crisis* 4 (June, 1912): 81.

[33] Seligmann, *op. cit.*, p. 152.

[34] Herbert J. Seligmann, *The Negro Faces America*, 2d ed. (New York: Press of Clarence S. Nathan, 1924), p. 299.

[35] Walter F. White, "Negro Segregation Comes North," *Nation*, 21 October 1925, p. 460.

Locke was interested in defining the "new Negro's" interest in his own culture in American terms; at the same time, however, he viewed the application of American ideals to black Americans as crucial to America's survival. "The Negro mind," he assured his readers,

> reaches out as yet to nothing but American wants, American ideas. But this forced attempt to build his Americanism on race values is a unique social experiment, and its ultimate success is impossible except through the fullest sharing of American culture and institutions.[36]

But the larger question facing America is the validity and vibrancy of democracy.

> Democracy itself is obstructed and stagnated to the extent that any of its channels are closed. Indeed they cannot be selectively closed. So the choice is not between one way for the Negro and another way for the rest, but between American institutions frustrated on the one hand and American ideals progressively fulfilled and realized on the other.[37]

The quality of life in America would surely deteriorate if the gap between her ideals and the reality continued to widen. Further, Locke suggested that if democracy failed to deal justly, black Americans would either become aggressively conscious of their blackness rather than of their being American, or they would become cynical, hateful, and indifferent. In either case, it would not auger well for America.

The most biting and ironic discussion of this subject occurred early in the century by Edward E. Wilson. In an article entitled "The Joys of Being a Negro," Wilson described the endless pleasures available to the black American. He had so much to look forward to because he had so little now. "With the Negro it is seldom that delights grow stale by being transformed from the imaginary to the real. . . . He had faith that the coming of his freedom would solve all questions for him; yet he found it but broadened his field of

---

[36] Alain Locke, "Enter the New Negro," *Survey*, 1 March 1925, p. 633.
[37] *Ibid.*

anticipation."[38] The Negro, he continued remorselessly, has the satisfaction of "knowing that the theory of things is right. In theory he has what any other man has; just as in theory all men are created equal—the law is impartially administered—we are a Christian nation."[39]

Thus, we come full circle. From a consideration in the previous chapter of the cheery words of advice of the *Southern Workman,* to the ironic tones of one commentator on the black man's status in America. All of the writers discussed in this chapter, with the exception of the Harlem culture critics, accepted the validity of the American value system and all desired to see its implementation for black Americans. Whether the writers spoke about self-help in economic terms or about adjustment to urban living, they used the language and the symbols of America. Whether they derided white America for failing a part of her own citizenry or whether they praised the concrete evidences of progress that blacks had made, they demonstrated a commitment to the American system. No foreign ideology was introduced; no appeal was made to un-American solutions. Success and progress were the magic words and the undying faith. Success and progress, in this best of all possible countries, could and would come to black Americans. This was the major message rising from the pages of black writings of the period. Psychologists and linguists inform us that the structure of our language governs our thought patterns. The Western dual perspective, of seeing things in terms of progress or regression, of darkness or light, has similarly influenced the American way of viewing the world. To black intellectuals, the North seemed immeasurably more hospitable to black people than the South; to black writers, progress was inexorable, even if it was erratic.

---

[38] Edward E. Wilson, "The Joys of Being a Negro," *Atlantic* 97 (February, 1906): 249.

[39] *Ibid.*

Chapter 4

Life in the North

The North was the promised land to southern blacks. It offered rural blacks big city living, jobs, and freedom from terror and lynching. While America was the golden land of opportunity to European immigrants, the cities of Chicago and New York were examples of mecca for southern Negroes. An Alabama woman wrote to the Chicago *Defender* that she wanted to take her children and leave "this dog hold because I don't know what I am raising them up for in this place and I want to get to Chicago where I know they will be raised and my husband crazy to get there because he know he can get more to raise his children...."[1] Despite the harsh winters and the alien environment, northern cities meant an escape from the boll weevil, the lynchers' rope, sharecropping, and a guaranteed unpleasant life. Southern Negroes from the Atlantic seaboard states migrated in large numbers to New York during the first thirty years of this century and were responsible for the development of Harlem into a huge black ghetto. Black southerners from the Deep South

---

[1] Quoted from a letter written on April 25, 1917, from Mobile, Alabama, and reprinted in *In Their Own Words: A History of the American Negro, 1916–1966*, ed. Milton Meltzer (New York: Apollo, 1967), p. 3.

moved to Chicago and Detroit. By 1928, almost a million and a quarter southern Negroes had migrated to the North.[2]

The Great Migration, as it was called, shifted the geographic focus of the race problem. No longer was it a purely southern problem; Negroes now lived north of the Mason-Dixon line in large numbers. The resulting race tensions and riots confirmed the southern whites' view that northern whites shared their racial attitudes. Blacks had to be taught to stay in their inferior place whether they lived in Birmingham or Chicago. If they did not, violence resulted. In the first twenty years of the twentieth century, there was at least one race riot every year with the number equally divided between the North and South. No section was immune.

Important and articulate black writers such as W. E. B. DuBois and James Weldon Johnson supported the promised land myth by affirming on numerous occasions that political power and greater economic opportunity *did* exist in the North for blacks; life may not have been idyllic in New York but it certainly offered more hope than did life in Mississippi. Throughout the twenties, for example, DuBois discussed the fact that Harlemites participated actively in local politics, voted discriminately, and elected black men to political office. Certainly no such claim could be made for Tuscaloosa, Alabama. Chicago provided another, perhaps more dramatic, example of black political participation.

Although Negroes constituted only seven percent of the city's population in 1930, there had been one Chicago Negro in the Illinois State Legislature continuously since 1882, two since 1914, three since 1918, four since 1924, and five since 1928. The first Negro alderman was elected in 1914 and the second one in 1918.[3]

In 1928, the First Congressional District in Chicago elected the first Negro to the U. S. House of Representatives since Reconstruction.

---

[2] There are many sources that deal with this general subject. Gilbert Osofsky's *Harlem: The Making of a Ghetto* (New York: Harper and Row, 1963) and Allan Spear's *Black Chicago: The Making of a Negro Ghetto, 1890–1920* (Chicago: University of Chicago Press, 1967) offer a great deal of information.

[3] James Q. Wilson, introduction to *Negro Politicians: The Rise of Negro Politics in Chicago* by Harold F. Gosnell (Chicago: University of Chicago Press, 1967), pp. vi–vii.

As DuBois noted in one speech, political power would not immediately "abolish color caste, make ignorant men intelligent or bad men good," but it is the "... beginning of all permanent reform and the only hope for maintaining gains."[4] Thus, the cities of the North offered political power to people who had been effectively disfranchised in their native areas. Moving to the North would not guarantee job opportunity or equality and it would not eliminate the color line, but it would provide the possibility to vote for and elect candidates that supported black needs. Because the reality of voting existed in the North, many black writers assumed that real power also existed. DuBois spent a great deal of time in the twenties trying to convince his black readers to vote independently. The gap between voting and significantly effecting major policy changes on the race issue was an entirely different matter. Black politicians played the game according to white rules and did not materially alter the race situation. Thus, a good deal of the supposed strength resulting from voting was fanciful.

But to articulators of the American Dream, such as James Weldon Johnson, the North was freer of race tension than the South. Writing in 1930, he observed that "more than 200,000 Negroes live in the heart of Manhattan, nearly a hundred thousand more than live in any southern city, and do so without race friction."[5] Johnson, a southern black who emigrated to the North early in the century, had positive experiences upon which to base his judgment. A successful song writer, poet, novelist, teacher, and field secretary of the NAACP, Johnson knew what struggle was, but he also had tasted success. His experiences accurately reflect those of the small but growing black middle class. With a college education, great ambition, intelligence, and hard work, a black man could achieve a measure of success in the promised land of New York. Harlem was "... a community in which Negroes as a whole are ... better housed than in any other part of the country," reported the Urban League in 1914.[6] New York had a major race riot in 1900 but after that, open violence did not occur. William Pickens's experience, which has already been described, paralleled Johnson's. While both men devoted their lives to the race issue and had much cause for dismay

---

[4] W. E. B. DuBois, "The Negro Citizen," *Crisis*, May, 1929, p. 155.

[5] James Weldon Johnson, *Black Manhattan* (1930; reprint ed., New York: Arno Press, 1968), p. 281.

[6] Osofsky, *op. cit.*, p. 111.

and discouragement, they also could display moments of hope and optimism based upon their personal achievements.

But to the overwhelming majority of black New Yorkers and Chicagoans, the North did not appear as the generous haven for the tired and oppressed of the land. The trade unions systematically prevented black entry. Kelly Miller observed early in the century that "the trade unions, either by the letter of the law or the spirit in which it is executed, effectually bar the Negro from the more remunerative pursuits of trade and transportation."[7] And Mary White Ovington, after conducting a study of New York black union men in 1906 concluded that only five percent of black workers were union members. Asphalt workers, teamsters, rockdrillers, tool sharpeners, cigar makers, waiters, and bricklayers constituted the only major unions that allowed black membership. None of the skilled trades such as iron workers, machinists, plumbers, or garment makers enabled black union participation.[8] To add insult to injury, Negro strikebreakers were used in seven major strikes in New York City from 1900 to 1920.[9] The situation was no different in Chicago.

Harlem became a slum during the very decade when its cultural accomplishments and cabarets became famous. During the twenties, as Gilbert Osofsky has aptly described, the tremendous increase in population through migration (115 percent, i.e., from 152,467 people in 1920 to 327,706 in 1930) created unbearably congested living quarters, rat infested houses, and a high tuberculosis rate.[10] Rents were high and going higher and black families were forced to take in boarders and have rent parties to meet the high cost of living. Whites left the neighborhood to avoid contact with the blacks but the houses they left were not sufficient to offset the great need. The infant mortality rate was shockingly high in Harlem, every kind of disease ran rampant, and crime flourished. The blues singing of Bessie Smith, the writhing of the black preacher, and the all-night drinking parties were expressions of the misery of life in the North. Every commentator on life among black New Yorkers has observed the abundance of churches in Harlem. "An

---

[7] Kelly Miller, "The Economic Handicap of the Negro in the North," *Annals of the American Academy* 27 (May, 1906): 84.

[8] Mary White Ovington, "The Negro in the Trade Unions in New York," *ibid.*, pp. 89–96.

[9] Osofsky, *op. cit.*, p. 42.

[10] Most of the material for this paragraph was obtained from Osofsky's chapter "Harlem Slum," *ibid.*

investigator found 140 churches in a 150-block area of Harlem in 1926."[11] Preaching a fundamentalist brand of religion, black ministers inveighed against evil rum, music, and theater. They preached an otherworldliness similar to their colleagues in the rural South.

James Weldon Johnson, among others, criticized the Negro church for its neglect of social issues. The Negro church, he argued, was a powerful force in the lives of black people and should use its influence to better social conditions for its congregation. "There is not now any other piece of organization machinery that could do these things as well as the Negro church could do them."[12] But the Negro Protestant churches, very much like their white counterpart, concentrated upon saving souls for the better life in the next world. This world was only a pale shadow of Heaven anyway and communal consciousness or reform could not wash away the sinfulness of each individual soul.

While the masses continued to occupy tenement houses, work in the most menial jobs of the city, and lead lives of quiet desperation, a black middle class grew. Harlem realtors such as Philip Payton, John Nail, and Henry Parker showed white America that blacks could own and manage property (although no more than twenty percent of Harlem was owned by blacks). Madame Walker, the cosmetics queen, displayed the conspicuous consumption habits of an upwardly mobile member of the nouveau riche. Black doctors and lawyers conducted business downtown as well as in Harlem, and black schoolteachers became conspicuous as did black workers in the post office and in other municipal departments. A significant black intellectual group also formed and became the basis of the Harlem Renaissance. For the first time in American history, a large number of educated, literate, and productive black Americans lived together in a congenial atmosphere, exchanged ideas, and generally constituted an intelligensia. They gathered at the home of James Weldon Johnson or at a cabaret and conducted the same variety of discussions that had characterized the salon of Mabel Dodge Luhan ten or fifteen years before. Black sociologists such as E. Franklin Frazier and Charles S. Johnson mixed and debated with poets Langston Hughes and Claude McKay and with novelists Rudolph Fisher and Jessie Redmon Fauset.

The staffs of the NAACP and Urban League provided many

---

[11] *Ibid.*, p. 144.
[12] Johnson, *op. cit.*, pp. 166–67.

members for this intellectual elite. NAACP members DuBois, James Weldon Johnson, Walter White, and William Pickens and Urban Leaguers Eugene Kinckle Jones and Charles S. Johnson all participated in the cultural life of Harlem. *Crisis* and *Opportunity* encouraged young black talent by publishing much of their poetry and short stories. Just as Greenwich Village had been an "interdisciplinary" intellectual community in the 1910s, so Harlem played this role for blacks during the twenties. In fact many Harlemites frequented the Village also. Claude McKay, for example, worked with white intellectuals on the staff of the *Liberator,* a radical Village magazine, in the early twenties. White and black intellectuals interacted both in the Village and in Harlem. McKay, in his autobiography, however, recounted one time when he took Oswald Garrison Villard to a favorite Harlem haunt of his only to be turned away at the door because of his white companion. But most of Harlem opened its doors to white customers, intellectuals or not. As Osofsky had observed, the gay side of Harlem life prevented any serious reform efforts of the seamy side. White intellectuals who frequented Harlem at night, and who only saw the glaring lights, the loud jazz bands, and the rhythmic dancing, knew nothing of ten people living in a two-room partitioned apartment.

The very fact that black intellectuals were both black and intellectual demonstrated the fundamental race problem and really dramatized the American Dream myth. The role of intellectual does not include any consideration of color; the role of the black man in America, whatever his intellectual attainments, very much does. Thus, while the American Dream legend emphasizes education as a crucial ingredient to socioeconomic mobility in this country, a characteristic the intellectual amply fulfills, the color line prevents the black intellectual from achieving the honored status to which his education entitles him. Black intellectuals, therefore, became conscious and concerned with their blackness and devoted their intellectual pursuits to this subject since they could never achieve the color-blind status of intellectuals in white America. Black intellectuals shared a life-style, value system, and world view with their white counterparts, but they did so *within* the confines of the black community and not in a truly interracial environment.

The two major black organizations, the NAACP and the Urban League, were also products of black life in the North. Although both groups addressed themselves to southern black problems, they both originated and gained most of their support and activity in the North. The Urban League, in fact, was created to deal with the immediate problems of adjustment that the southern blacks faced in their new environment. This kind of effort aptly typifies the good hearted actions taken by the wealthier, settled members of a particular minority group toward their less fortunate brothers. It confirms the existence, of course, of a stable black middle-class community in cities such as New York. City governments in 1900, 1910, or 1920 did not provide housing, job opportunities, or unemployment insurance for new arrivals. German Jews established agencies to help their newly arrived landsmen, and New York City blacks did the same for their southern brethren. The Urban League acted as the middleman to southern migrants just as the settlement houses had at the turn of the century for European immigrants. For many disoriented blacks in Chicago or New York, the Urban League provided the same services as Hull House or the Henry Street Settlement House.

Both organizations operated very much within the American Dream frame of reference. They implicitly and explicitly shared the goals and attitudes of the dream. They demonstrated, often quite dramatically—and tragically—their faithful reliance on the efficacy and validity of the dream. The NAACP and Urban League exemplified the power of the dream on organizations as well as individuals. Just as individual black leaders were products of the dream, so were black organizations. By reading their own progress reports, analyzing their activities, and listening to their own views, one clearly sees their commitment to progress, almost an inevitable progress, within the political, economic, and social structures of our society. Paradoxically, the American framework provided both the strength and weakness of these organizations. On the positive side, because the black organizational leaders shared the value system with white America, they could speak the same language, communicate mutually understandable values, and state their case in mutually acceptable terms. But herein lies one major difficulty: white America's fundamental unwillingness to include blacks in the basic society precluded a meaningful dialogue.

Black leaders believed that the methods as well as aims of liberal democracy would be a viable foundation upon which to erect the desired society. They thought that when the white power structure, as well as the ordinary citizen, learned of the injustices suffered by black men, this discovery would become the basis for remedial action. This faith, the essential faith of all American reformers, often proved unfounded. For example, Lincoln Steffens, an urban muckraker of the period, came to realize, much to his shock and dismay, that exposing corruption did not lead inevitably to its eradication. So too in the case of the race problem. The NAACP and Urban League strove valiantly to inform and acquaint the American people with the enormity of the discrimination against black Americans. But the successful creation of awareness did not lead to corrective action.

The black leaders of these organizations operated continuously within the guidebook of the establishment. They fervently believed in the concept of progress, in the inevitable advances that black America would make, and in the good will of many white people. As a result of this perspective, success was often defined as existing with very modest evidence to support it. As has already been noted, the *Crisis* would often report the minutest actions as evidence of significant achievement. The fact that a total of over thirteen thousand black women voted, for example, in the states of California, Colorado, Idaho, Utah, Washington, and Wyoming in 1912 was cause for rejoicing.[13] The fact that a white philanthropist, Julius Rosenwald, donated funds for black schools in the South received frequent mention in the black periodicals and claims for progress far beyond their accomplishments. The counterevidence, massive disfranchisement of black voters in the South and the inadequate public funding of education, was discussed, of course, but the modest evidence of good news was supposed to balance effectively the large doses of bad news.

The black organizations and their leaders were trapped by their own ideology. The notion of progress is seductive and all encompassing. It creates a self-fulfilling prophesy. If you believe in progress, you believe that you see evidence of it in every time and place. W. E. B. DuBois, as editor of *Crisis* during the period under study, was the captive of this idea. Although he vigorously criticized the white American failure to live up to her own ideals, he also noted the evidences of progress and continuously encouraged his black brothers to keep up the good work. The inevitable tension of observing failure and progress simultaneously must have caused him

---

[13] News item, *Crisis* 5 (November, 1912): 7.

immense frustration. Eugene Kinckle Jones, the executive secretary of the Urban League during most of the twenties, was another example of an ardent spokesman for the American Dream. His yearly progress reports unfailingly reflected his firm belief in the steady improvement of the black man's status.

"The Association began with appeals to law enforcement authorities," declared Herbert Seligmann in his review of the twenty-year achievements of the NAACP,

and to public sentiment for a minimum of decency and human justice. It developed into a fact-finding instrument....[14]

"Appeals" to law enforcement agencies to carry out their functions and pleas to the public to display a "minimum of decency and human justice" sound pitifully bland from the perspective of the 1970s. But they accurately reflect the frame of reference within which intellectuals in the early part of this century operated. After all, these were the only methods approved and known to the educated elite that governed the NAACP. Relative to the past, also, the NAACP was a major step forward. Herbert Seligmann, for example, had been a reporter who investigated race conditions in the South during the 1910s and early 1920s; after he joined the staff of the NAACP as director of publicity, he saw what he considered significant progress in the lives of black Americans, especially in the North, in the middle and late twenties.

In fact, Seligmann's book, *The Negro Faces America*, published in 1920, was one of the first major efforts to bring the dilemma of black Americans before a general white audience. In this study, Seligmann displayed the typical temperament and outlook of a reformer. He considered rational analysis the first step in any endeavor and assumed that the truth will free people and lead them away from erroneous actions.

If Negroes were conceived to be human beings like any other human being, educable and educated, adapted to the processes of American government and appreciative that liberty for oneself

---

[14] Herbert J. Seligmann, "The NAACP Battle Front," *ibid.* 36 (March, 1929): 83.

implies liberty for others, Negro domination would have no immense terrors.[15]

The problem with this statement, and much of Seligmann's analysis
of the situation, is the *a priori* assumption that underlies it: to wit,
that reasonable people accepting the reasonableness of this view,
would behave reasonably. Of course, the statement begins with the
word "if." Because Negroes were not considered fundamentally the
same as white *Homo sapiens,* the whole comment topples down.
There is also the undying faith that logic prevails in human thinking and that liberty for one and all means precisely that in every
mind that considers the subject.

Unfortunately, these assumptions did not accurately reflect (and
still do not) white American thinking. But the whole thrust of the
NAACP rests upon this very assumption. Seligmann's mode of analysis was not unique to him. It was shared by DuBois, James Weldon
Johnson, Walter White, Mary White Ovington, and Oswald Garrison Villard, to name but a few of the leaders of the NAACP. The
leadership of the Urban League, even more consciously geared to
sociological analysis and investigation, shared this intellectual orien-
tation. To put it another way, the programs, plans, and tactics of the
NAACP and Urban League demonstrated their implicit devotion
to the American Dream myth, to the view of progress, and to the
belief in the human ability to define a problem and devise a solution
to it.

It has already been suggested earlier that the tremendous interest
in black education and black economic progress expressed a fundamental acceptance of the myth. But even more than that, it showed
that an enormous problem, such as the race problem, could be
dissected into its major parts with each part carefully analyzed,
corrected, and then returned to the whole. Obviously, a great problem can only be handled when it is narrowed down into controllable
units. Woman's freedom is defined and translated into a program
for suffrage; black emancipation is interpreted to mean the vote,
jobs, housing, and education. Similarly, the black organizations
divided the race problem and tried to deal with specific parts of
it with the implicit hope that when all of the parts had been suc-

---

[15] Herbert Seligmann, *The Negro Faces America,* 2d ed. (New York: Press
of Clarence S. Nathan, 1924), p. 11.

cessfully accomplished, the whole would be organically sound. The implementation of this principle is evident in the stated purposes of each of the black organizations: The NAACP concentrated on legal means to upset segregation, while the Urban League used social workers to aid black laborers in adjusting to city life. Each organization attacked one segment of the huge and difficult problem of race discrimination.

Clearly, a set of priorities is also implicit in the particular objectives of the respective group. The NAACP interpreted legal discrimination to be the primary monster that had to be conquered before black Americans could enjoy equal opportunity in America. The Urban League, on the other hand, was formed by sociologists such as Jones and Charles S. Johnson and they viewed the social adjustment of blacks into urban life as most crucial. Thus, they centered their energies and programs on the attainment of their distinctive goal. The unspoken hope of the black organizational men was that each group operated on a parallel, but mutually constructive, course and that if, and when, each did its particular job well, the race problem would be solved.

Therefore, success, a very American goal, was measured by each organization within the limited areas to which they addressed themselves. For example, in 1929 the NAACP, in reviewing their major accomplishments after twenty years of existence, pointed to four major victories at the Supreme Court level: the overturning of the Louisville segregation case, the Arkansas Peonage cases, the Louisiana segregation case, and the Texas white primary. They also cited their anti-lynching campaign as one of their most significant successes.[16] Since the NAACP program revolved around legal battles in the courts, they pointed to these specific successes as the concrete evidence of their accomplishments. Indeed, these decisions established legal precedents that would aid the battle against segregation in the future. But their successfulness in the context of the twenties is more doubtful. With the benefit of hindsight, of course, these positive gains seem modest. Political disfranchisement in the South remained until the 1960s; the same is true of residential segregation in the country as a whole. However, the NAACP cannot be faulted for their few examples of concrete action. The courts and the whole legal system were the

---

[16] Seligmann, "The NAACP Battle Front," *op. cit.*, pp. 97–98.

traditional and accepted means of accomplishing desired change. Judicial action, combined with journalistic appeals, seemed to be the only course open to reformers. Legal justice still remains the primary means of affecting social change.

Eugene K. Jones's analysis of the accomplishments of the Urban League after fifteen years reflect the same basic style. Jones noted the development of forty-two local leagues, the work of the league's department of research and investigation, the training of social workers, and the numerous conferences held as evidence of the major advances made by the league.[17] Once again, the reader is faced with what appears to be limited gains. The enormity of the problem, however, could not be adequately encompassed in the program and agenda of two organizations. The leaders of both groups fully appreciated this point at the same time that they hoped that their particular work would accomplish a larger good. In a sense, the NAACP and the Urban League, two small parts in a very large whole, hoped to equal more than the sum of their parts. This inarticulated hope probably characterizes many American reformers who work through specific organizations. The desire to work on a concrete level but achieve on a higher, abstract level created an unresolvable dilemma that reformers interested in making broad changes in their society must experience. During the early years of this century, both the NAACP and Urban League could point to modest gains in their respective areas. Relative to the bleak past, the future appeared hopeful. In addition, given their utter faith in the viability of the dream for black Americans, they viewed their successes as part of the inevitable improvement of race relations in America.

Reference has been made to the sociological bent of the Urban League. (DuBois, of course, was also a trained sociologist.) This intellectual frame of thinking assumes that rational analysis of a problem, based upon empirical investigations, will lead to an effective solution. This mode of thought is scientific and very American. It also leads to another view; namely, that *an* organization can contain a total problem, that is, with the proper tools and methods, a major, complex problem can be effectively solved. In the 1910s, it appeared that the race problem could be effectively

---

[17] Eugene Kinckle Jones, "The Fifteenth Year," *Opportunity* 3 (March, 1925): 81–83.

defined and dealt with in this way. For example, Eugene K. Jones observed in 1916 that Brooklyn had developed an effective program for helping black migrants. A day nursery, a staff of social workers, and a babies' welfare association had all been formed.[18] In other words, a vital plan had been implemented to deal with a concrete problem. And all enlightened people could applaud the Urban League's efforts and achievements. The black population in Brooklyn was modest and could be handled.

The mass migration to Harlem in the twenties disarmed the League. They simply could not deal with the numbers of newly arrived blacks from the South and the West Indies. Thus, according to this view, the method of analysis employed by the League was not faulty; however, the sheer numbers of people with whom they had to deal was too formidable for them. Also, much of their support was in small black communities, rather than exclusively in Harlem and/or Chicago. There were simply not enough professional black social workers to staff these desirable agencies. Further, white assistance, in terms of money and professional services, was urgently needed. The Urban League, although dependent upon some white support, enlisted support within the black community. This fact points to another dilemma: if you express the issue in terms of race, and try to get blacks to solve their own social problem, you release the whites from responsibility—when they were primarily responsible for creating the problem.

The NAACP's tactics and strategy also were valid. But the nature of attacking specific laws in specific cities made the task enormous. There were many Louisvilles in America. There were many devices to restrict black voting in the South other than the white primary. To institute legal suits against each and every one was impossible. Just as enough day nurseries could not be created to meet the increasing problem of black migrations, so enough law suits could not be started to deal with the massive discrimination blacks faced everywhere. One of the key difficulties faced by the black organizations during the first thirty years of this century was the enormity of the problem certainly and the lack of needed resources, especially white aid to deal effectively with it.

---

[18] Eugene Kinckle Jones, "Negro Welfare," *Survey,* 30 December 1916, pp. 371–72.

The legal thrust of the NAACP, and it was the only significant legal defender of black Americans during this period, cannot be underestimated. However, the modest victories in the courts in areas such as voting rights, restrictive covenants, and residential segregation ordinances did not have the power to overturn the abuses in each of these areas nationally. They did not achieve what a class action suit hopes to achieve; the reason for this is that the Supreme Court did not view segregation as inherently unequal. The major judicial breakthrough that the NAACP needed, but did not achieve during this period, was to obtain the acknowledgment from the Court that any governmental action that discriminates is implicitly unconstitutional. Until that acknowledgment was made, each Louisville residential segregation ordinance, each white primary law, and each example of violation of due process, had to be attacked and argued in terms of the particular situation under review. Thus, the procedure and the goal of the NAACP was not in error; rather, the error lay with the point of view of the conservative Supreme Court of the United States.

All reform organizations faced another distressing concern that may be inescapable. When reading *Crisis* and *Opportunity*, one is continually reminded of the preacher who criticized his congregation for not attending church faithfully. He misplaced his criticism. The people who should hear his sermon were at home and were not interested. Similarly, articles in the black magazines often were addressed to the very people who did not read the magazines. Civil rights advocates tried to appeal to racists when their readers, who shared their philosophy, were already civil rights advocates. Those who did not accept the humanness of the blacks did not read the black magazines, would certainly not contribute to the NAACP, and assiduously avoided reading anything that would change their minds. Thus, a limited audience of readers was exposed to material that confirmed their beliefs. This, in itself, is a fine attainment. However, it does not achieve the prosyletizing motive of the organizations. If changing attitudes is one of the major objectives of the black organizations, they were not successful. They did not recruit or exploit new markets for their "product."

Many of the NAACP's and Urban League's weaknesses and failures were inherent in the nature of things. That is, because they accepted the values of the culture, they operated within the framework of the culture. This is as it should be if we accept the essential validity of the American Dream and only criticize its limited application. One of the supposed strengths of the American Dream, however, is its dynamism, responsiveness, and flexibility. The concept of movement and motion is part of it—both individual motion and group motion. The American system is supposed to be accommodating and aware of the demands of each interest group in its citizenry. According to this interpretation, once black Americans organize, articulate their grievances in a proper and respectful way, and call attention with concrete evidence to instances of injustice, the system will correct itself. It will absorb the dissidents and remedy the ills.

This was the overriding hope of the NAACP and the Urban League. Unfortunately, it was not fulfilled. But the evidence suggests that the responsibility for the failure must lie with the insincerity of the established white powers. The black leaders observed the proper formula, followed the correct procedure, and remained loyal to the objectives of the system. The brightness of the American Dream began to fade by 1930 for many black American leaders. The economic depression of the previous year surely contributed to the disillusionment. But the essential conclusion had to be that what was an attainable dream for one portion of the American population was a mockery for black Americans.

Chapter 5

The Irony of the Dream

The imaginative writings of the period truly capture the terrible irony of the American Dream for black Americans. In fiction, a writer can portray contrasts and heighten tragedy. The black writer used his medium to express the gap that existed between the professed ideals of America and the unpleasant reality for black Americans. In poetry, short stories, and novels, the writers reminded their readers of the promise of America and her broken promise to a significant segment of her population. *Crisis* and *Opportunity* and, to a lesser extent, the "white" magazines encouraged imaginative black writers and often printed their work. Both *Crisis* and *Opportunity*, for example, had annual poetry and fiction contests. The poetry of the best black poets of the twenties was published first in the black magazines. Poems by Langston Hughes, Countee Cullen, and Claude McKay appeared frequently in *Opportunity*. The short stories of Jessie Fauset were found in *Crisis*. Miss Fauset, whom we will discuss later, was the book editor of *Crisis* also. The popular white magazines would occasionally publish a short story by Rudolph Fisher and a poem of Hughes. But the bulk of black fiction was published in the black periodicals.

In the succinct and cogent form of a poem, a writer could, and did, often capture the essence of the American tragedy in race relations. James David Corrothers, for example, a black poet of the period, now forgotten, but praised by his black contemporaries as one of the ablest poets of the black race,[1] wrote poems for *Crisis* as well as the popular white magazine *Century*. Corrothers described in his poetry the woeful discrimination blacks suffered every day in America. "At the Closed Gate of Justice" effectively expressed the sadness, the rueful endurance, and the incredible patience that characterized the life of every black American. "To be a Negro in a day like this," the opening line of each verse, was followed by a sorrowful description of the humiliation of blackness. To be a Negro demanded forgiveness, patience, and loyalty, according to Corrothers; truly, these were virtues that blacks had had many years to develop and thus had in ample quantities. His final verse asks the Lord for an explanation, for surely no man has one. But, he concludes, "I pass by, the glorious goal unwon. 'Merely a Negro'—in a day like *this!*"[2]

Corrothers's poetry often expressed a sardonic humor and tongue-in-cheek playfulness. His white audiences who read his poetry in *Century* magazine appreciated, I am sure, the double entendre in his poems. In "An Indignation Dinner," Corrothers described a Christmas season in a small town where the black people had been having hard times. They wanted to have a fine holiday dinner but did not have the means of obtaining it. The white employers were stingy and the blacks were without resources. So the black workers had a secret meeting and decided to take a fat turkey from a "certain gemmun's fahm." They voted, befitting proper democratic procedure, to take it and so they did. "*Not* beca'se we was dishonest, but *indignant*, sah. Dat's all."[3]

Using the tools of democracy, these blacks practiced direct action and out of indignation acted in their own behalf. The message was clear. As one speaker in the poem said: "Ef you'd keep a mule a-wo-kin, don't you tamper wid his oats."[4] When white men sub-

---

[1] DuBois described Corrothers as one of the two greatest living black poets (Braithwaite was the other one) in "Men of the Month," *Crisis* 9 (January, 1915): 116.

[2] James David Corrothers, "At the Closed Gate of Justice," *Century* 86 (June, 1913): 272.

[3] James David Corrothers, "An Indignation Dinner," *Century* 91 (December, 1915): 320.

[4] *Ibid.*

ject blacks to economic and political servitude, black endurance
is not infinite. To more impatient black poets of the twenties,
most notably Claude McKay, Corrothers stretched the limits and
was willing to endure far more injustice than he could, or would.
But Corrothers, in this sense, occupied a transitional position; his
poetry dealt with black themes, recognized the gap in treatment
between whites and blacks, but did not assume a militant stance
or tone.

The ideals of democracy, the values that white America held
dear, and the frequent protestations of white virtue were favorite
themes in black literature. How could it be otherwise? The titles
alone of some of the poems of the period effectively demonstrate
the point: "Lincoln Monument," "Our Land," "The White Ones,"
and "America," all by Langston Hughes. "Freedom" by Henry
Reich, Jr., and "Democracy" by A. Aloysius Greene demonstrate
the obvious preoccupation with the theme of America's ideals. The
poignancy and emotion that blacks experienced is laconically en-
capsulated in such verses as "Democracy":

> The scene: a crowded subway train
> At the close of a busy day.
> Blue-blood hob-nobs with plebian,
> Wending their homeward way.
> The milling, pawing crowds push in,
> Some treading on my feet;
> While on either side of small brown me,
> Remains an empty seat.[5]

The two best black poets of the period, Langston Hughes and
Claude McKay, often dealt with the theme of America's hypocrisy.
Hughes's "America" won third place in *Opportunity's* poetry con-
test for the year 1925. The poem begins by describing the polygot
assortment of people who make up America: the little dark baby,
the little Jew baby, the little outcast. The blue-eyed, the crinkly-
haired, and the blonde-haired children all compose the essential
population of our land. Together, he continues, we are one. "You
and I./And I?" he asks ironically. "Who am I?" and with this

---

[5] A. Aloysius Greene, "Democracy," *Crisis* 36 (May, 1929): 160.

question he proceeds to describe the history of the black American; he reminds white Americans of Crispus Attucks, Jimmy Jones, and Sojourner Truth's roles in the building of America. "Today's black mother bearing tomorrow's America." The black American, Hughes goes on to say, dream the dream of America, hope, pray, fight, and know that "There are stains/On the beauty of my democracy...." He concludes the poem with this identification of himself: "I am my one sole self,/America seeking the stars."[6]

The history and life's blood of the black American is inextricably tied to the history and life's blood of the white American, according to Hughes. The destinies of both populations are interlinked. The dreams of America are dreamed by both races. The striving for the fulfillment of America's beautiful ideals is deeply felt and desired by black Americans. At the same time that Hughes eloquently sang of the unique virtues of black people, he iterated and reiterated the theme of oneness of all Americans, or rather the extreme need to make her one. In "Lincoln Monument," Hughes tersely, though fondly spoke of Old Abe who sits "lonely in the marble and the moonlight," alone and quiet, "and yet a voice forever...."[7] Abraham Lincoln, the Great Emancipator, was being ignored. His loneliness depicted America's gross neglect of the race problem. But patient Old Abe would endure. This certainly seemed to be implied in Hughes's poem. The meaning of his actions and the larger meaning of America demanded action.

Claude McKay, a Jamaican emigre to these shores, participated in the Harlem Renaissance and was one of its brightest lights. Although his residence in America was brief during this period, his poetry powerfully expressed the wounds of injustice and discrimination that characterized the life of black Americans. "America in Retrospect," for example, portrays the feelings of a person who has been deeply wounded by the marred vision of America. First, America puts forth "gorgeous pageants" for her viewers to see but is blinded by her own "Shadow" which besmirches the earlier vision. But the speaker feels no hatred "For you make me a stoic introvert," and he can now devote himself wholeheartedly to writing "in freedom and peace/ The accumulations of the years

---

[6] Langston Hughes, "America," *Opportunity* 3 (June, 1925): 175.

[7] Langston Hughes, "Lincoln Monument," *Opportunity* 5 (March, 1927): 85.

that burn/ White forge-like fires within my haunted brain."[8] Once again, America presents a dream to her citizens that entices them and that they believe in, only to be dashed if the believers' color is black. The dream motif is dominant and persists in much of the literature. The horrible chasm between the ideal and the real, the dream and the actuality, a favorite theme of writers, is effectively expressed.

One final poetic example, "A Thorn Forever in the Breast" by Countee Cullen, another major black poet of the twenties, also captured the dream theme. The subject of the poem cannot rest because his heart "is loyal to the least of dreams;/ There is a thorn forever in his breast/ Who cannot take his world for what it seems."[9] Irony of all ironies. This person, who still believes in a grander dream, cannot accept the ugliness of the world around him. He cannot face the falseness of reality but must persistently hope that it will yield more than meets the eye. His doom is predetermined. His eternal fate is misery. Once again, the black American is portrayed as the unhappy captive of a dream that is unattainable. Life becomes an unending exercise in frustration. What should be and what is can never be merged. America's rhetoric can never become reality for black America.

The black poets of America, writing in the first third of this century, and most especially in the 1920s, understood the terrible dilemma facing black Americans. They believed in the dream and its validity. They hoped that America could be forced to own up to her heritage. Often, as has been suggested, they argued that the destiny of America would be determined by whether she, in fact, faced her race problem. Her future, and these words may have been prophetic if there was to be a future, demanded a positive bridging of the gap between the American Dream and the American reality for black Americans. "To Negroes," a poem written by an obscure poet named Howard J. Young, effectively described this theme:

> You who carry
> The lance of laughter and the sword of song,

---

[8] Claude McKay, "America in Retrospect," *Opportunity* 4 (November, 1926): 342.

[9] Countee Cullen, "A Thorn Forever in the Breast," *Opportunity* 5 (August, 1927): 225.

Let this be blazoned on your pennons:
Whatever the color of man,
The shadow must always be black.[10]

America could never survive, let alone survive in a healthy and vibrant way, black poets kept saying, until she faced the falseness of her words and ways. The beauty of America was her hopes and visions for her citizens; her destruction would be based precisely on her unwillingness to carry out her own promises.

The short stories of the period also dealt with this theme. Rudolph Fisher, a black doctor who returned to Harlem in the early twenties, published a few stories in the *Atlantic Monthly* that demonstrated his concern for this crucial subject. In both "The City of Refuge" and "The Promised Land," Fisher depicted New York, and especially Harlem, as the promised land for black Americans. Southern blacks, as well as West Indian blacks, migrated to Harlem because it was supposed to be the fulfillment of the American Dream, black American style. But, as the grandmother said in "The Promised Land," "... a 'promis' land.' All hit do is promise."[11] Economic opportunity, mobility, and a lack of discrimination were all part of the wish; but Harlem did not fulfill the promise; its internal struggles and intense hatreds demonstrated the lack of unity within the black community. Fisher's stories depicted Harlem as the setting for serious quarrels between northern blacks, southern blacks, and West Indians. It also turned out of be a haven for dope peddlers, gangsters, and hucksters. The evils of the city, Fisher implied, far outweighed their supposed virtues. And blacks, especially from the South, were no match for the sharpshooters from Harlem and Jamaica. Conniving blacks were the villians in these pieces, not the hypocritical whites. But the dream of success in Harlem was one variation of the larger theme, a variation, however, that grimly portrayed the factionalism and viciousness within the black community.

One of the most popular subjects for black fiction was the mulatto —after all, what better symbol existed for the inextricable tie, the absolute interrelatedness that obtained between the black man and

---

[10] Howard J. Young, "To Negroes," *Opportunity* 4 (January, 1926): 15.

[11] Rudolph Fisher, "The Promised Land," *Atlantic Monthly* 139 (January, 1927): 41.

the white man? The mulatto was the living example of racial co-existence. He was the breathing sign that blacks and whites could, and did, live together. Yet—and here the tragedy deepens—neither race accepted him. The mulatto, although the living proof of sexual compatibility, was the rejected person. He was literally and symbolically the black sheep in the family. Further, he often self-consciously separated himself from his blacker brothers, only to be rejected by the whites. One of the first prominent black writers in America recognized the dilemma of the mulatto. Charles Chesnutt, himself a mulatto, achieved prominence as a black writer at the end of the last century. He often spoofed the snobbish mulattoes who would not admit their blackness. One of his mulatto characters, for example, explained his fate thusly:

> Our fate lies between absorption by the white race and extinction in the black. The one doesn't want us yet, but may take us in time. The other would welcome us, but it would be for us a backward step.[12]

Another protagonist, Mr. Clayton, in the story "A Matter of Principle," analyzed the situation in this way:

> I know that the white people lump us all together as Negroes, and condemn us all to the same social ostracism. But I don't accept this classification, for my part, and I imagine that, as the chief party in interest, I have a right to my opinion. People who belong to the most virile and progressive race of modern times have as much right to call themselves white as others have to call them Negroes.[13]

Booker T. Washington also accepted the implicit assumption that the white race was the most progressive and therefore that their standards were the best. White is right, a sardonic reminder of the power and influence that the dominant whites possessed over blacks, became a favorite satirical theme in black writing. During the Harlem Renaissance of the twenties, many black writers urged their black readers to reject whiteness as a goal and to be proud of their blackness. Langston Hughes, most notably, preached this

---

[12] Charles W. Chesnutt, *The Wife of His Youth and Other Stories of the Color Line* (New York: Houghton Mifflin, 1899), p. 7.

[13] *Ibid.*, pp. 94–95.

point of view. But the mulatto was a tragic figure. American society asserted, in every facet of its culture, that whiteness was desirable and that blackness was evil. Therefore, at first, the mulatto could rejoice at the lightness of his skin. But when he discovered that white America fastidiously rejected anyone who had even a taint of blackness in his complexion, he was tormented. His psyche had to take quite a beating. If he consciously accepted his blackness and lived as a black man, he would often become bitter, confused, and alienated. He did not question the white culture's standards, only its unwillingness to include him. This was one path many mulattoes followed.

Other mulattoes, such as the Blue Vein Society people, described in one of Chesnutt's stories (they were so light skinned, you could see the blue veins in their foreheads), consciously separated themselves from their darker brothers, imitated the habits and snobbish customs of the white society, and waited for the day when white America would take them in. Still others, of course, positively identified with their blacker brothers and tried to elevate them. In much of the fiction of the period, in fact, there is the implicit, if not explicit, assumption that the mulatto was a cut above the ordinary black man, and it was his obligation to help the less fortunate blacks. In the novels that we will discuss, the heroes were mulattoes who felt that it was their duty to uplift their blacker brothers. Indeed, most of the real life "heroes" and leaders of black America were mulattoes.

"Passing" was also a favorite theme. Light-skinned men and women would often pass into white society rather than suffer at the hands of discrimination. In the typical plot on the subject, there was always the moment of discovery when whites realized that they had, mistakenly of course, allowed a black person into their midst. This could result in tragedy if the light-skinned person had been a young woman preparing to marry a very eligible white man. Or it could result in the light-skinned person proudly asserting his true identity and emerging chastened but more virtuous from the experience.[14]

"Emmy" by Jessie Fauset, for example, is a story about a dark-skinned girl whose sweetheart, Archie, is a very light mulatto.

---

[14] Chesnutt's "House Behind the Cedars" illustrates the first tragic consequences of discovery while "Emmy" by Jessie Redmon Fauset illustrates the second result.

"Archie's clear olive skin and aquiline features made his Negro ancestry difficult of belief."[15] Emmy, a sweet, well-bred girl, has only experienced a minimum of discrimination in her life due to color. Her boyfriend, ambitious and interested in getting ahead, discovers that he can pass into white society. He gets a job in a different city and lives in a white world. When Emmy comes to visit him and they are observed together by his boss unexpectedly, the boss assumes that he is sporting with this black girl. Archie is torn between his desire to keep his good job, his love for Emmy, and his wish to marry her and to acknowledge publicly his color. After a falling out between the couple and some further tribulations, they are reunited, the truth is told, and everything ends happily—Archie keeps the good job, marries Emmy, and lives openly as a Negro. Miss Fauset seemed to be saying in this story that honest mulattoes will be accepted on the basis of their merit and that they do not have to hide their identity—a typically romantic American view that ignores cold reality.

Taken objectively, the black writer faced a difficult, if not insoluble, problem in dealing with his subject matter. On the one hand, he wanted to portray the stark existence and the horrible discrimination that pervaded the life of every black American, North and South. On the other hand, he also wanted to project a favorable image of the black man to his white readers so that they would be sympathetic to his plight. If black people were shown to be virtuous, hard working, and courageous in fiction, then white America would treat blacks humanly in real life. Thus, the theme of discrimination was often coupled with characterizations of black people that made them infinitely patient, perseverant, and kind. No matter what rank injustice they experienced, they suffered in silence or bounced back in a manly but legal, nonviolent way. In the novels of the period, especially, the black protagonists rarely if ever ranted and raved over their fate; rather, they proudly faced the world and continued to knock their heads against the wall of prejudice.

The American Dream was also a central theme in many of the novels. *The Fire in the Flint* (1924), written by Walter F. White, the field secretary of the NAACP, was considered one of the major fictional efforts of the decade. Jessie Redmon Fauset's *There Is Confusion* (1924) also was rated highly by her contemporaries. *The*

---

[15] Jessie Fauset, "Emmy," *Crisis*, December, 1912, p. 80.

Blacker the Berry (1929) by Wallace Thurman, a bright but brooding light of the Harlem scene, received mixed reviews but was readily acknowledged as an important contribution to black literature. None of these novels are literary masterpieces, but they are representative of the novels of the twenties as well as significant illustrations of how the dream theme was used by novelists. I will also compare these novels to T. S. Stribling's *Birthright* (1922). Stribling, a southern white man, was considered a sympathetic observer of the race problem in America and wrote extensively on the subject. Further, Jessie Fauset claimed that she wrote *There Is Confusion* after having read *Birthright* and concluding that a black writer could treat the subject of race relations better than any white writer.

Despite Miss Fauset's view, the two books are more alike than different in theme and characterization. In both *There Is Confusion* and *Birthright*, the protagonists are mulattoes who are well educated but who cannot cross the color line regardless of ability. In Stribling's novel, Peter Siner, a Harvard graduate (how much "whiter" can you get?), returns to his home town, Hooker's Bend, Tennessee, to discover that white prejudice applies to him as well as to all of his illiterate black neighbors. In Miss Fauset's novel, Joanna Marshall, the heroine in the story, is an accomplished singer and dancer who discovers, once she tries to enter the entertainment business, that her color is a decided obstacle. As a matter of fact, when she began formal studies in dance with one of New York's finest instructors, he agreed to teach her privately or with a few of her friends, but not in an integrated class. But to Joanna, this was not a humiliating price to pay—just as long as she could study dance. Only later, when she wanted to display her talents and receive her just rewards of fame and fortune, did she realize the horrible role color played in determining people's destiny.

Walter F. White's *The Fire in the Flint* also described the life and problems of a well-educated mulatto, Dr. Kenneth Harper, who was educated in a fine northern school, interned in New York City, and served in the army in France. When he returns to Central City, Georgia, after the First World War, he too finds that racism and the traditional separation of the two races prevents any kind of communication based upon human qualities. Both White's and Stribling's novels are set in the South, while Fauset's is in New York City. This is a significant point which is reflected in the story line. Joanna Marshall in *There Is Confusion* does not really experience discrimination in a dramatic and total way until late in the novel. Most of the story describes her growing up in a prosperous home (her father was a successful caterer) surrounded by many friends. It is only when she tries to begin a professional career that she encounters bias. Eventually, it should be added, she succeeds, especially among the arty Greenwich Village types who considered a mulatto singer and dancer a major asset in the late twenties.

Dr. Harper and Peter Siner experience the senseless hatred and violence of prejudice almost upon their arrivals in their respective southern home towns. Harper tried to remain aloof from the race problem but his younger, more militant brother continuously harangued him. Dr. Harper tried to follow the advice of his father, who had been well regarded by the white community in town; the late Mr. Harper's philosophy, which clearly endeared him to the whites, was succinctly quoted by his son: "Any Negro can get along without trouble in the South if he only attends to his own business."[16] Dr. Harper finds that it is impossible to heed this advice especially after he falls in love with a young lady who is morally outraged by the injustice and miserable treatment experienced by the poor black farmers in the area. Before long, Dr. Harper is organizing a farmers' cooperative (the idea was his girlfriend's) and he is clearly on his way toward extinction by violence in this deeply southern town.

Peter Siner also tried to help the poor, uneducated blacks in his community; he hoped to buy land and build a school for black children. But Henry Hooker, the town banker, deceived him and wrote an exclusion clause in the real estate contract which prevented blacks from going on the property. So, less than a week back from Harvard, Peter's hopes for uplifting his black brothers were dashed. It is only in this book, written by a white man, however, that an explicit reference is made to the fact that the protagonist (as well as his girlfriend, Cissie Dildine) is of mixed blood, and the reference is derogatory to the blacks:

> It was the white blood in his [Peter's] own veins that had sent him struggling up North, that had brought him back with this flame in his heart for his own people. It was the white blood

---

[16] Walter F. White, *The Fire in the Flint* (1924; reprint ed., Westport, Conn.: Negro Universities Press, 1969), p. 17.

in Cissie that kept her struggling to stand up, to speak an un-broken tongue, to gather around her the delicate atmosphere and charm of a gentlewoman. It was the Caucasian in them buried here in Niggertown.[17]

This feature of *Birthright* ties it to the traditional white treat-ment of the subject: the acceptance of whiteness and the whole white value system as superior in every way to black. Further, it demonstrates the incredible arrogance of white Americans. Neither Dr. Kenneth Harper nor Joanna Marshall ever say anything like this. But, and here is a crucial irony, they do accept, implicitly, the whole structure and culture of white America. They do operate within the American Dream frame of reference; Kenneth and Joanna accept education, talent, skill, and hard work as important and proper ways of accomplishing great deeds. They believe, as all Americans believe, that by following the proper formula, they will obtain their due reward. They desire the material and spiritual benefits deserving of accomplished behavior. And they believe, most ardently, that America is the country of fair play, mobility, and opportunity. Further, both black authors may implicitly share at least a part of Stribling's explicit reference because their respec-tive heroes are mulattoes—not black, black men. Thus they may also share, albeit unconsciously, the color code that says that white is right and the blacker you are, the less civilized you are. But they do not attribute their ability or motivation to their white blood.

At one point in the novel, Joanna's brother-in-law states what appears to be Miss Fauset's basic views on the subject of race in America:

But every colored man feels it sooner or later. It gets in the way of his dreams, of his education, of his marriage, of the rearing of his children. The time comes when he thinks, "I might just as well fall back; there's no use pushing on. A colored man just can't make any headway in this awful country." Of course, it's a fallacy. And if a fellow sticks it out he finally gets past it, but not before it has worked considerable confusion in his life.[18]

---

[17] T. S. Stribling, *Birthright* (New York: Century, 1922), p. 98.

[18] Jessie Redmon Fauset, *There Is Confusion* (New York: Boni and Liveright, 1924), p. 179.

With love and patience, the author says elsewhere, the determined and able black man can achieve success in America. But only after confusion and tremendous perseverance and effort. The novel ends in typical American fashion, on a basically optimistic note. Like her short story, "Emmy," Miss Fauset believed that the basic worth of people, combined with the fundamental sense of fair play of white Americans, will enable all worthy people, despite their color, to succeed.

Not so with the other novels. *The Fire in the Flint* ends violently with Dr. Harper being killed by the Ku Klux Klan. The Klan had been outraged by his efforts to organize farmers and his supposed fraternization with a white woman. Even before his violent end, however, Kenneth Harper began to doubt the efficacy and validity of American democracy. He ruefully commented to a white man whom he was treating for syphilis:

> If this thing called democracy that I helped fight for is worth anything at all, it ought to mean that we coloured people should be protected like anybody else.[19]

(This is also a nice bit of irony as this prominent white man could not go to the white doctor in town under these circumstances, so Dr. Harper, the black man, became suddenly qualified to treat a white man.) While discussing the race problem with white liberals in Atlanta, he also indicated a sense of the extreme complexity and difficulty on the subject of democracy:

> You see, we're in the habit of thinking that we can find a simple A-B-C solution for any given problem, and the trouble is there are mighty few that are simple enough for that.[20]

Dr. Harper's girlfriend, Jane, expressed the most militant statement in the book:

> No race in all history has ever had its liberties and rights handed to it on a silver platter—such rights can come only when men are willing to struggle and sacrifice and work and die, if need be, to obtain them![21]

---

[19] White, *op. cit.*, p. 68.

[20] *Ibid.*, p. 253.

[21] *Ibid.*, p. 179.

The American Revolutionaries of 1776 would probably agree but southern white Americans would not—neither would twentieth-century northern white Americans, for that matter.

Each of these quotations effectively represent often stated themes on the race issue. First, the reminder that democracy must guarantee some protections for all of her citizens. Secondly, the American view that there is an A-B-C solution to all problems is questioned by Harper. This belief is expressed in a conversation with white liberals, not avowed racists. The eagerness of the whites to know the answer to the race problem accurately depicts the frame of thinking and the temperament of many white reformers. Walter White, in his role as field secretary and later executive secretary of the NAACP, must have spent many hours talking to and working with the same kind of white liberal reformer. And finally, Jane's willingness to sacrifice anything and everything for the race struggle typified the feelings of impatient blacks who had given up waiting and hoping for gradual change. It is interesting to note that this view is expressed by a woman who, by her own admission elsewhere in the book, is ineffectual. Women, White may be saying, express the most extreme, emotional positions—positions not articulated (but possibly believed?) by the respectable black men.

Peter Siner, in *Birthright*, leaves Hooker Bend a depressed and defeated man. He and his new wife, Cissie, go to Chicago where Peter had been promised a good job. Life in the North, Stribling suggested, for an educated mulatto was quite decent. In the South, however, neither the illiterate blacks nor the racist whites could, or would, accept advice or consider changing their respective ways. The impetus for Peter's reformist tendencies, his white blood, would help him adjust to urban living in the North, but was totally unsuitable to the setting in which he was born and raised. The doctrine of racial differences, with the white race possessing all of the superior and adaptable traits necessary for survival, pervades the whole novel. The tragedy of Peter Siner, in Stribling's terms, is his mixed blood—not the horrible and unjust way that people are divided according to color. This fact, ultimately, provides the major distinction between a white novelist's and a black novelist's treatment of the race subject. Dr. Harper dies in the South while serving his community and Joanna Marshall finally achieves success on her own terms. So while the black writers share in the belief that the mulattoes are the natural leaders (and natural superiors?) of their blacker brothers, they have their protagonists remain true to their convictions and callings. They do not pass for white; neither do they desert their people. Joanna Marshall does not emigrate to Paris and Dr. Harper does not move to New York. They accept themselves and their respective roles in black society. Their lighter skin enabled them to gain an education and to advance in society; now, they would apply their advantages to help less fortunate blacks.

Thurman's *The Blacker the Berry*, (the title was taken from a Negro folk saying "The blacker the berry/the sweeter the juice") concerns itself with the personal struggle of one Emma Lou, a black girl born and raised in Boise, Idaho. Emma Lou had the unfortunate fate of being born dark skinned in an extremely color-conscious family. Emma Lou's grandmother in particular, the matriarch of the family, placed a great deal of stock in marrying lighter-skinned men and thereby whitening the family. Her daughter defied her, married a dark-skinned man, and produced Emma Lou. The man eventually left but Emma Lou stayed, the constant reminder to her socially striving family that they were, in fact, black people. The whole story concerns Emma Lou's tormented internal and external wanderings. From Idaho, she goes to college in Los Angeles, only to be excluded from the society of the other black students because of her color. Harlem then calls and the rest of the story deals with her difficulties there. She has some inconsequential love affairs, falls in love with a light-skinned ne'er-do-well, whom she supports, leaves, and eventually returns to. Finally, after many tortuous experiences and attempts to come to grips with her color and herself, Emma Lou leaves Alva, her philandering boyfriend, and resolves to discover who she is and what she wants out of life.

Thurman's story, in contrast to the others described, deals entirely with black society. White America never enters into the dilemma. The frustration and lack of identity become purely internal matters to be resolved within the black community. Emma Lou's self-hatred led her to frantic and frequent attempts to lighten her skin. (Her hair was her one redeeming characteristic: it was wavy and luxuriant.) Emma Lou's blackness made her struggle one of gaining acceptance into desirable black society. Her education and family upbringing created attitudes of contempt for "common" black folk. She had the family status and educational accomplishments to qualify for elite black society, but because her skin was darker than the mulatto minority that ruled, she could not attain social equality. In Harlem, the sporting people to whom she was attracted shared the values of the mulattoes and rejected her, or at best used her. At one point in the novel, she turned away from the bohemian group, attended church, finished her schooling so that she could teach, and joined the respectable middle class. But she found these people banal; she yearned for the gay life. While the "respectable" blacks accepted her, she always doubted their sincerity and did not enjoy their company.

Thurman's portrayal of Harlem revealed his critical appraisal of all black society. The educated were dull; the lively were dissipates; and the overwhelming majority were bland. Color snobbishness reigned supreme and none of the accepted means of social advancement were meaningful. Thurman seemed to be rejecting the American Dream for black society and in so doing rejected black society, since it accepted that dream. The shallowness and escapism of Harlem life, its utter meaninglessness because of the extreme preoccupation with the color issue, led nowhere. Emma Lou resolved to try and define her life at the end of the novel. Whether she succeeded or not, the reader never knows. Given her options, as described in *The Blacker the Berry,* her chances were slim. In a review of the novel for *Crisis,* DuBois judged it a failure in execution although the theme, he thought, was a good one.

> And above all, the author must believe in black folk, and in the beauty of black as a color of human skin. I may be wrong, but it does not seem to me that this is true of Wallace Thurman. He seems to me himself to deride blackness.[22]

The self-despising of Emma Lou, DuBois suggested, may have been Thurman's disease. The bleakness of the novel, surely, repelled DuBois. While the editor of *Crisis* still believed in creating authentically whole black personalities within white society, Thurman seemed to question that goal. There is no solution in *The Blacker the Berry;* there is no realistic hope of improvement. Clearly this book had to be one of the most subversive statements regarding the American Dream. As long as color prejudice existed, and it seemed to be eternally persistent, healthy black men could not be created. While Fauset envisioned hope and White exhibited healthy outrage, Thurman painted a dark and pessimistic picture.

---

[22] W. E. B. DuBois, untitled book review, *Crisis,* July, 1929, pp. 249–50.

Walter White and Jessie Fauset portrayed the humanness and the universality of human traits in black people. According to any and all rational and empirical standards of judgment, there was no difference between Joanna Marshall and Isadora Duncan. Dr. Kenneth Harper could be any young white doctor beginning his medical career. His education, value system, and manner of speech and dress put him into the same category as all white doctors—and yet, because of the pigmentation of his skin, his life was doomed. Emma Lou, her family, and the larger black society had so effectively internalized its hatred for blackness that its dark-skinned members could not achieve a viable identity. All of the characters' chances for human success were severely diminished. By taking educated mulattoes, as Fauset and White do, people who subscribe in every material way to the white American standard of excellence, the black novelists have shown the absurdity of discrimination and the hypocrisy of American ideals. Indeed, *There Is Confusion* and *The Fire in the Flint* effectively portray both the allure of the American Dream and its failure to include black Americans.

The First World War, the war to make the world safe for democracy, also received attention in some of these novels. As discussed earlier, the ironic gap between making the world safe for democracy and making America safe for blacks, could not be ignored or overlooked. Dr. Harper noted that black Americans were discontented after the war and wanted more because they had fought

> not so much because they were fired with the desire to fight for an abstract thing like world democracy, but, because they were of a race oppressed, they entertained very definite beliefs that service in France would mean a more decent regime in America, when the war was over, for themselves and all others who were classed as Negroes.[23]

In Stribling's *Birthright,* Tump Pack, a black war hero who returned home on the same train as Peter Siner, marvelled at the fact that he had received a Congressional Medal of Honor for killing "fo' white men." "Yas-suh," Tump continued, "I never wuz mo' surprised in all my life dan when I got dis medal fuh stobbin fo' white men."[24] But

---

[23] White, *op. cit.,* p. 43.
[24] Stribling, *op. cit.,* p. 12.

Peter, the Harvard graduate, assured him that it was all right since:

> You were fighting for your country, Tump. It was war then; you were fighting for your country.[25]

The ironic twist here is apparent. I wonder whether Stribling recognized the possibilities of his own statement. Is it proper to fight for your own rights as well as your country? The implications are positively subversive.

Thus, these representative novels of the twenties on the race issue, with the exception of *The Blacker the Berry*, described educated black men trying to operate within the white American scheme. Thy were always hampered and often decisively defeated. Walter White dramatically expressed life in Central City, Georgia, with lynching being the standard way that whites kept blacks in their place and in which raping black girls was a normal pastime. *The Fire in the Flint* was the only novel discussed that dealt with the dilemma of southern blacks and the viciousness of southern whites in stark and realistic terms. The novel caused quite a sensation and was considered good propaganda for Walter White's and the NAACP's crusade against lynching. But the profound terror that filled the life of the southern black was not captured in the novel; the brutality of the black man's experience in the South and its most vivid and literarily excellent portrayal became a major theme a generation later in the writings of Richard Wright. In the twenties, the novelty of White's book and its sensational character excited some discussion but was quickly forgotten as an exaggerated and overheated account. No one could be more American than Langston Hughes was when he described the motley assortment of human beings who came to these shores in search of a better life. No one could accuse Jessie Fauset of other than American goals when she suggested that the doors of opportunity should be opened impartially to all who were qualified to enter. No one could deny that democracy meant equal treatment of all human beings before the law. Thus, the imaginative writings, whether they were poems, short stories, or novels, expressed the dominant theme of the American Dream. The experience of reading about discrimination and the failure of the dream in a fictional context may have created

---

[25] *Ibid.*

more sympathy with the problem, but it certainly did not alter material conditions.

Some black literary critics believed that the "so called" Negro renaissance was more superficial than real. Wallace Thurman, for example, labeled many of his colleagues banal and sentimental; he also felt that many black writers pandered to white tastes and portrayed blacks as sociological problems rather than as human beings.[26] In Thurman's mind, good literature, good black literature, had to depict the blackness of blacks as well as the humanness of blacks. In other words, it had to be both universal and particular. The vitality and reality of black life had to be colorfully portrayed as well as the essential humanity of all blacks. It is interesting to test Thurman's literary criterion on *The Blacker the Berry*. I think I would have to agree with DuBois that Thurman's characterization seems to suffer because of his own confused doubts. Also, the characters in his novel are not unique personalities but rather shallow stereotypes. Thus, as apt as Thurman's criticism was of much of black literature in the twenties, his own work was not free of the same problems.

Langston Hughes and Claude McKay, according to Thurman, were the only two black poets who fulfilled his criteria. Claude McKay's poem "If We Must Die" typified the kind of true protest poetry Thurman wanted to see emerge from black writers:

> If we must die, let it be not like hogs,
> Hunted and penned in an inglorious spot . . .

Thurman viewed Countee Cullen, another popular contributor to the Harlem Renaissance, as insipid. He found Walter White and Jessie Fauset to be weak writers who presented stereotypical portraits of black people.[27] In Thurman's eyes, Dr. Harper and Joanna Marshall were too pure to be human. The need to portray blacks as wholly virtuous and to assign all evil traits to white men struck him as being singularly unrealistic. Given the propaganda aim of these writers, of course, it is understandable, albeit not good art.

---

[26] Wallace Thurman, "Negro Artists and the Negro," *New Republic*, 31 August 1927, pp. 37–39. See also Thurman, "Negro Poets and Their Poetry," *Bookman* 67 (July, 1928): 555–61.

[27] Thurman, *op. cit.*

As discussed earlier, George Schuyler also disputed the worthiness of much black writing. His major criticism, however, was not literary and esthetic but philosophical. Schuyler denied the existence of a separate black culture and therefore questioned the validity of uniquely black writing. He rejected the idea of peculiar, unique features of black writing although he too contributed novels to the period's literature.[28] Indeed, the discussion of whether there was such a thing as a black culture was crucial to a discussion of black literature. If one took the position that the life of a black American was substantially no different from the life of a white American, then you could not produce a separate literature based upon racial differences. Without entering the argument directly, the black writers of the period accepted the difference of blacks and proceeded to demonstrate how the life experiences of a black man in America differed from white men.

In all of the fiction discussed in this chapter, color did become the determining factor in the lives of all the fictional characters. The context and framework of each story may have appeared to be no different from any other story but the significant variable that affected the destiny of all the people was race. This fact could not be avoided or overlooked. Thus, the standard goals, plots, and characters of a piece of black fiction lost their standard and conventionality when viewed in terms of race. Dr. Kenneth Harper's life ended tragically precisely because he was black; and Peter Siner left his home town because his color prevented him from achieving his life's hope. The poetry of Langston Hughes frequently reminded the readers of the irony of words such as democracy and equality when spoken by unequally treated black men.

Undoubtedly, all, or many of the black writers, contributed imaginative works that did not deal specifically with the race issue. Countee Cullen's poetry, for example, often expressed typical poetic sentiments about spring, sunshine, and other generally acceptable poetic subjects. Black writers did not write about race all of the time. Neither did they discuss the irony of the American Dream consistently. But this theme did occupy much of their thinking and writing. I would also argue that the most potent and dramatic writing of the period dealt with the dream concept. The seemingly unbridgeable gap between the ideals of America and the ugly reality

---

[28] See references on pp. 42–44.

for black Americans was not only a favorite theme of black writers; it was one that never lost its relevance during this whole period. It described, in the most realistic terms, the actual life situation for most black Americans, and in this way, qualified as being literature *verité*.

The black writers faced a serious internal identity crisis during the 1920s. With the influx of West Indian blacks as well as southern blacks into Harlem, the question Who is a black American? became difficult to answer. Writers concerned with depicting the life and thought of their people found that the portrait of blackness was not a uniform or homogeneous one. Country bumpkin blacks mixed uneasily on the streets of Harlem with sharpshooting Harlemites and Jamaicans. Thus, the black writers found that their view had to encompass a very diverse group of black people. Most of the novelists of the twenties, however, dealt with the problem by ignoring it; they wrote about the middle class, the settled blacks of America. Jessie Fauset's protagonists were wealthy black Philadelphians. Some writers chose to romanticize the gaiety and drama of life in Harlem. With the exception of Wallace Thurman, the image of Harlem and black America is one of fun. Claude McKay's *Home to Harlem*, James Weldon Johnson's *Black Manhattan* (non-fictional), and Nella Larsen's novels portray New York City blacks in a jocular manner.

The North generally received better notices as home for black people than the South. Walter White's *The Fire in the Flint* vividly attests to the black view of the South. The fictional artists, therefore, shared many of the same perceptions with the organizational leaders and the black intelligensia in general. Just as the treatment of the Negro problem in the factual literature existed within the frame of reference of Americanism, so the fictional writers followed the same pattern. This aspect of the imaginative writings of the Harlem Renaissance has never before received serious attention or seen within the larger context of the period. Journalists and poets shared the same view: betterment for black Americans was attainable in this best of all possible worlds and the North held ·the promise. American rhetoric adequately expressed black American goals and the need for the future was to translate the words into reality.

Chapter 6

Rejectors of the Dream

So far, we have described and analyzed the way in which black writers operated within the American Dream context—both in factual reports and fictional works. The framework of gradualism, progress, and desirable, if not inevitable, evolutionary change has informed all of these writings. The subject of this chapter veers sharply away from this dominant mode. The rejectors of the dream do just that—they repudiate both the world view that pervades the American Dream myth and the means of attaining it. Some of the rejectors, however, base their views on the meaninglessness and utter irrelevance of the dream as applied to black Americans. That is, they may not deny the validity and desirability of the dream, but they state, quite emphatically, that it is a white man's dream and one which was never intended to apply to black Americans. Marcus Garvey best represents this view. To Garvey, a Jamaican, blacks could never hope to participate in the abundance of America. In his native land, light-skinned Negroes were used by the white powers to manage their affairs and their black men, but no black man, however light, could expect equal opportunity at the hands of the white man. Surely, the majority of dark-skinned blacks, argued Garvey, were doomed to inevitable servitude in white America.

Other critics argued that the American Dream was misleading

and did not accurately reflect or describe reality in America—for the majority of blacks *and* whites. Those who held this view, usually espousers of Marxism, discussed how few Americans have been upwardly mobile and have benefitted economically and socially. In the land of infinite opportunity, these critics pointed out, the rich have been getting richer and the poor, poorer. Opportunity and mobility are fictions and the capitalistic structure must be transformed to effect true social equality and economic opportunity. Further, many of the repudiators had little patience with gradualism, legislative reform, and evolutionary change. They spoke in terms of revolution, and not evolution. Not only were the goals of the American Dream unacceptable, but also the methods were impotent. New legislation could not deal with the inequities that existed.

Who are the rejectors of the dream? During the period under study, they are not many relative to the number of articulate black writers who operated within the dream context. Usually, they wrote for small radical magazines located in New York City and were not known outside of that metropolitan area.[1] This presents a problem in discussing them. Most of these magazines had very short-lived publishing careers. The *Messenger,* the magazine of Socialists A. Philip Randolph and Chandler Owen, is perhaps the best known leftist journal and the one most readily available. However, some of the more obscure ones, such as the *Crusader,* the organ of the African Blood Brotherhood, and the *Challenge,* edited by William Bridges, are hard to come by. Scattered copies exist in the Schomberg Collection in the New York Public Library and nowhere else.

The popular magazines of the period had occasional references to black radicalism which we will discuss but the subject was not comprehensively treated. One could argue that this fact properly reflected the minimal role radical literature played. But clearly, other interpretations could also be made from this conspicuous lack of data. DuBois offered some editorial comment on the subject in *Crisis,* and the Lusk Committee, the Joint Legislative Committee of the State of New York Investigating Seditious Activities, had a

---

[1] In one survey of black leadership, Abram Harris noted: "The Communist element makes its appearance as the latest development in racial leadership. At present its following is quite small and its voice is hardly heard outside New York City" (Harris, "The Negro Problem as Viewed by Negro Leaders," *Current History* 18 [June, 1923]: 410–18).

chapter on "Propaganda Among the Negroes." From these diverse sources, therefore, some analysis can be made of the ideological content of black radicalism. That is our main concern in this chapter: to see in what ways black writers departed from the American Dream context and what they provided as the philosophical and rhetorical framework for their views.

Black American radicals believed that the color line made the Declaration of Independence and the Constitution white men's documents. They firmly felt that however noble America's principles were, they were not directed to, or for, black Americans. Marcus Garvey, and the mass movement he inspired, adhered to this point of view. Garvey did not repudiate capitalism or its attending virtues of hard work, thrift, individual success, and mobility. He did not reject gradualism as a value. He simply did not believe that biracial harmony was possible anywhere in the world. Thus, the goal of black Americans, according to Garvey, was to separate from white America—either by leaving for Africa or by creating a wholly separate black community in this country. As a West Indian emigre to this country, Garvey's experience had taught him that the color white stood for colonialism and exploitation of blacks; never could, or would, color prejudice disappear. Thus, Garvey was a rejector of the American Dream—or perhaps more appropriately, he challenged the applicability of the dream for black Americans. As has already been suggested, the Founding Fathers did not include black Americans in their promises. It has only been in the twentieth century that black and white leaders have used the original principles and documents of America to argue for equality of the races. Marcus Garvey had not been raised on the beauty of American rhetoric and he found the words of the Declaration hollow and hypocritical.

The popular magazines in the twenties had frequent pieces on Marcus Garvey. He was good copy. His colorful uniforms, parades in Harlem, and grandiose business schemes attracted a great deal of attention. Two different magazine writers labeled him the "Negro Moses"[2] and indeed, to many of his followers, he must have seemed to be the deliverer of the black masses from their serfdom. The Universal Negro Improvement Association, the Black Star Line, the

---

[2] T. H. Talley, "Marcus Garvey: The Negro Moses?," *World's Work*, December, 1920; and Rollin Lynde Hartt, "The Negro Moses and His Campaign to Lead the Black Millions into Their Promised Land," *Independent*, 26 February 1921.

Back to Africa scheme, and the Negro *World*—all Garvey produc-
tions—inspired confidence; in 1919, Garvey claimed that his association had thirty branches in this country and over four million
members. These figures may be exaggerated but Garvey's following
surely ran into the hundreds of thousands. He appealed to the
ordinary, inarticulate black man, not the literate intellectual group
that read *Crisis* and *Opportunity*. In fact, the light-skinned leadership of black America, typified by DuBois, was Garvey's archenemy.
Garvey's Jamaican experience had taught him that mulattoes were
often treacherous middlemen who compromised and exploited their
blacker brothers for pieces of silver from the white man.

DuBois, of course, discussed Garveyism in the pages of the *Crisis*.
Generally, his analysis was temperate and fair. In his first discussion of Garvey in December, 1920, DuBois characterized Garvey as
a sincere, dynamic, and honest man but one who has serious de-
fects of "temperament and training: he is dictatorial, domineering,
inordinately vain and very suspicious." But he is "an extraordinary
leader of men. Thousands of people believe in him."[3] DuBois defined him as the leader of the West Indian emigres who had come
to America to improve their lot and had a difficult time adjusting to
the urban environment. In a second article the following month,
DuBois described in detail Garvey's business enterprises, primarily
his ship line, the Black Star Line. Here he discovered bad business
methods, vague financial reporting, and plain inefficiency. DuBois
noted that Garvey had "spent more for advertisement than he has
for his boats!" But once again, DuBois did not dismiss Garvey entirely. He agreed that black capitalism was a desirable, and feasible,
goal for black Americans. He supported the black efforts to organize
their own industry and to join hands with Caribbean blacks for the
eventual goal of redeeming Africa. However,

> ... it will take for its accomplishment long years of painstaking,
> self-sacrificing effort. It will call for every ounce of ability, knowl-
> edge, experience and devotion in the whole Negro race. It is not
> a task for one man or one organization, but for co-ordinate effort
> on the part of millions.[4]

---

[3] W. E. B. DuBois, "Marcus Garvey," *Crisis* 21 (December, 1920): 60.
[4] *Ibid.* (January, 1921): 114.

DuBois's main objections to Garvey were his bombastic personality, his wild exaggerations, and his unwillingness to cooperate with
the existing black leadership in New York. "American Negro leaders
are not jealous of Garvey—they are not envious of his success; they
are simply afraid of his failure, for his failure would be theirs."[5]
DuBois recognized the exciting mass appeal of Garvey and the real
contrast between his charismatic personality and the staid, rational
approach of the NAACP and Urban League leadership. He believed
that there was room for both approaches. However, he did not fully
appreciate the extent to which Garveyism was removed from the
mainstream of American life, or rather, the extent to which Garvey's
emotional appeal rejected the system and values of America. Perhaps this is the enigma and the paradox of Garveyism: its methods
were conventionally within the American capitalistic system but its
cry of black separatism and black power rejects the theoretical color
blindness of America. Whether or not America practices what she
preaches is not at issue here; it is simply what she preaches. And in
the twentieth century, according to most of her black and white
spokesmen, the American message is equality before the law regardless of color. Garvey rejected this goal because he believed pro-
foundly that it would never be practiced.

In an article for *Century* magazine on Garvey, DuBois unknow-
ingly stated the dilemma. He acknowledged the fact that: "Deep in
the black man's heart he knows that he needs more than homes and
stores and churches. He needs manhood—liberty, brotherhood,
equality," and he ends the piece with "which path will America
choose?"[6] What is suggested here is that DuBois framed the psychic
needs of black men *in terms of* the American frame of reference. He
viewed liberty, brotherhood, and equality within the value system
of America. Garvey, I am arguing, did not see the desired goal that
way at all. (Whether he was fully aware of this or not, I do not
know, but it seems safe to assume that he consciously rejected all
the symbols and values of America.) Garvey's goal of brotherhood
would be of the brotherhood of black men; his concept of liberty
was for a free black Africa and his notion of equality was of black
leaders dealing equally with white leaders. Marcus Garvey did not
want or expect to achieve any of these goals within America. If

---

[5] *Ibid.*, p. 115.

[6] W. E. B. DuBois, "Back to Africa," *Century* 105 (February, 1923): 548.

black Americans remained physically on this continent, it would still be as a separate cohesive unit and not as an integrated group into the mythic American melting pot. To DuBois, equality, liberty, and brotherhood would be, or rather could be, achieved in America—the vision was a genuine biracial, bicultural America. Black *and* white together. To Garvey, separate but equal was the desired goal.

Charles S. Johnson, editor of *Opportunity*, generally agreed with the DuBois analysis of Garveyism. He added, however, another explanatory element. To Johnson, the new psychology provided insights into the phenomenon of Garvey. "The compensatory value of dreams" became Johnson's major reason for Garvey's success. Economically and socially deprived blacks dreamed of bettering themselves in this country where progress is promised to all. Because their wishes were not fulfilled, they dreamed and had a rich fantasy life. Garvey supplied them with beautiful dreams and hopes. "Balked desires, repressed longings, must have an outlet." Johnson noted that the black man's discontent must be dealt with or the blocked off dreams will take another direction. "Perhaps," he ended rhetorically, "this also will be harmless. But who knows?"[7]

Professor Kelly Miller of Howard University, usually considered a moderate, if not extremely conservative, black leader of the period, provided one of the most astute analyses of Garvey. Writing in 1927, when Garvey was in jail on charges of mail fraud, and his movement languishing as a result, Miller praised Garvey's efforts at creating race pride—a goal Miller had been advocating for years. He also credited Garvey with having spoken to lower-class blacks, a group that the black intellectuals had conspicuously ignored. Further, he touched upon the essential difference between Garvey and the rest of the black leadership in America when he said of his colleagues:

> Their whole teaching is based upon equality of the races which they hope to enforce by appeal to the white man's conscience, reason and aroused sense of righteousness. Mr. Garvey believes that the racial prejudice of the Anglo-Saxon is so deeply imbedded in acquired emotions, if not in natural instinct, that no amount of moral suasion or coercive force which the Negro can

---

[7] Charles S. Johnson, "After Garvey—What?," *Opportunity* 1 (August, 1923): 232–33.

command, will have any sensible effect upon it. . . . He looks upon the struggle for racial equality as futile and hopeless.[8]

This is the only statement by a contemporary of Garvey that approaches the interpretation that I am arguing. Miller, however, does not carry it through to its logical conclusion. Perhaps he was afraid of confronting the starkness of the position or its radical implications.

Sociology professor Miller, whose whole world view was based upon reason, careful investigation before making a judgment, temperate analysis, and patience, perceived the emotional and philosophical chasm that existed between himself and Garvey. Clearly, Marcus Garvey's temperament, his excesses, and his wild generalizations and claims were the antithesis to the way the black leadership in America approached a problem and dealt with it. But more fundamentally, Garvey rejected reason and moral suasion as methods of obtaining justice, and in so doing rejected the very foundation of reform in America. Social change in this country occurs, according to the official view, through the system with the methods of propaganda, moral pressure, and education. Black and white reformers have held firmly to this view. It is an article of faith in American democracy. Thus, Garvey's utter repudiation of these methods, his replacement of them with direct action by blacks to better their own lot and to remove themselves from white America, was clearly a stinging indictment of the American system.

Of all the contemporary accounts on Garvey, only one argued that he was not a radical at all. Abram Harris, a young writer, social worker, and economist, contended that if Garvey had been a radical, he would have been summarily deported during the First World War period along with white radicals. Garvey, he argued, "did not plan the destruction of a government in America, but the construction of one in Africa." Garvey preached that this is a white man's country, cooperated with the Ku Klux Klan, and approved of Jim Crowism. Thus, Harris said, he was not radical. He did not threaten the sanctity of private property; according to Harris, Garvey's failure to win over the black intelligensia and middle class was due to their own view that they were acculturated. "They were fighting for

---

[8] Kelly Miller, "After Marcus Garvey—What of the Negro?," *Contemporary Review* 131 (April, 1927): 496–97.

civil and social recognition as American citizens and were little concerned with an African empire. Not so with the bulk of Garvey's followers."[9] Harris then characterized the adherents of Garveyism much like other commentators had; they were poor, alienated, seeking a better life, and were unconcerned with the practicality of Garveyism. According to Harris's view, the only possible form of radicalism is communism because it threatens the economic and political structure of American society. Whether Garvey was a radical or not is not as crucial a distinction for this analysis as the fact that he rejected the American Dream. Essential to the American Dream is followers who believe, with an undying faith, in its worth and relevance. Marcus Garvey never accepted the dream. It is not clear whether his followers shared in his rejection. Perhaps they attended Garvey's meetings, contributed to his schemes, and still adhered, implicitly, to successful adjustment in America. Marcus Garvey may have provided good escapist entertainment, as many of his contemporary critics suggested, for poor black people.

The Marxists rejected both the American Dream and Garveyism. A. Philip Randolph, one of America's leading black Socialists in the 1920s, entitled one article on Garvey, "A Supreme Negro Jamaican Jackass."[10] Randolph, a believer in class consciousness rather than color consciousness, argued that Garvey was unrealistic and wrong headed. In a series for the *Messenger*, the journal Randolph co-edited with Chandler Owen, Randolph refuted Garveyism; he saw the taking over of Africa from the white colonialists to be a vain and arrogant dream. "Conquering Africa is not any less difficult than conquering Europe."[11] He argued that "black despotism is as objectionable as white despotism."[12] Moreover, Randolph objected to the fact that Garvey was uninterested in dealing with the black American problem in the context in which it occurred—in America. "Everything which is done in America is done with a view to hastening the exit of the Negro from America. . . . This is why Mr. Garvey does not advise his non-citizen followers to become citizens of the United States."[13]

[9] Abram L. Harris, "The Negro Problem as Viewed by Negro Leaders," *Current History* 18 (June, 1923): 416–17.

[10] A. Philip Randolph, "A Supreme Negro Jamaican Jackass," *Messenger* 5 (January, 1923).

[11] A. Philip Randolph, "The Only Way to Redeem Africa," *ibid.*, p. 569.

[12] *Ibid.*

[13] *Ibid.* 4 (December, 1922): 541.

Finally, Randolph's major criticism of Garvey was his failure to appreciate the proper source of the black man's troubles in America.

> Garveyism will not only not liberate Africa, but it will set back the clock of Negro progress by cutting the Negro workers away from the proletarian liberation movement expressed in the workers efforts, political and economic, to effect solidarity, class-consciousness, by setting them against, instead of joining them with, the white workers struggle for freedom. Herein lies the chief menace of Garveyism.[14]

In an article entitled "Should Marcus Garvey Be Deported?," Chandler Owen, Randolph's coeditor on the *Messenger*, answered an emphatic yes. "Every self-respecting Negro," he continued,

> is called upon to rescue the race from the Black Kluxer's disgrace. Garvey must get out of Negro life everywhere. There is no place in America for a black race baiter, one time reviling all white men; and a "good nigger" race traitor, at another time selling out the rights of all Negroes.[15]

Although Randolph repudiated Garveyism, he shared with him a common rejection: the American framework and analysis of social evils. The Socialist-Marxists, then, became the other major group in the 1910s and 1920s who found the American Dream wanting and devised an alternative solution to the race problem.

A spectrum existed, however, in the radical Marxist group. W. E. B. DuBois considered himself a Socialist but a moderate Socialist relative to A. Philip Randolph. Everyone left of DuBois did not consider him a radical in good standing. But, as will be shown, he did share many views with the more extreme Socialists. Randolph, on the other hand, was temperate relative to William Bridges or Cyril Briggs. Thus, a variety of opinions, and, perhaps even more to the point, a variety of temperaments characterized the Left. Randolph considered himself a scientific Socialist as did DuBois but the former talked in terms of the class struggle and doctrinnaire socialism while the latter stressed the ability to succeed within the non-

[14] A. Philip Randolph, "Black Zionism," *ibid.* (January, 1922): 335.

[15] Chandler Owen, "Should Marcus Garvey Be Deported?," *ibid.* (September, 1922): 480.

violent and pragmatic framework of America's judicial and legislative system. Hubert H. Harrison was a doctrinnaire Socialist while Briggs and Bridges often coupled their Marxism with discussions of color prejudice.

Usually in discussions of black radicalism in the twenties, Randolph and Chandler Owen and their magazine the *Messenger* provided the major evidence. This is because it seemed to have the largest circulation of a Socialist journal in New York and had the greatest effect. Contemporary magazine accounts of black radicalism also pointed to the *Messenger* as the best example of this genre. In Abram Harris's survey of black leaders in 1923, his whole discussion of "Negro Marxians" is on Randolph and Owen.[16] Similarly, E. Franklin Frazier's analysis in 1928 called the *Messenger* editors the New Radicals.[17] Frazier characterized the *Messenger's* philosophy as being economic in origin and being a forceful repudiation of the old guard black leadership. The *Messenger* advocated the use of the strike and retaliation against lynching. The Socialist magazine counseled black men to resist the draft during the First World War and claimed that one-fourth of the Negro voters in New York supported the Socialists in 1917.[18]

In sharp contrast to the reluctant support that DuBois gave to the war effort and the positive assurance of patriotism that most black leaders provided, Randolph and Owen totally rejected the validity of the war aims for black Americans. "The Huns of Georgia are far more menacing to Negroes than the Huns of Germany."[19] The black Socialists scoffed at the Wilsonian ideals and rejected the League of Nations. Chandler Owen labeled it "The League of White Capitalist Governments," and continued the critique by saying that it was "against the peoples of all the nations. . . . It is the Capitalist International suavely and subtly set forth in saccharine language."[20] Making the world safe for democracy was a hypocritical goal in light of the black man's reality in America. In the September, 1919, issue of the *Messenger*, the editors included two articles that indi-

---

[16] Harris, *op. cit.*, p. 414.

[17] E. Franklin Frazier, "The American Negro's New Leaders," *Current History* 28 (April, 1928): 57.

[18] *Ibid.*, p. 58.

[19] Editorial, "The Crisis of the Crisis," *Messenger* 2 (July, 1919): 11.

[20] Chandler Owen, "The League of White Capitalist Governments," *ibid.* (June, 1919): 17.

cated the new mood of radical black Americans. One editorial entitled "If We Must Die" (after Claude McKay's poem) discussed
the Chicago and Washington riots and concluded that the New
Negro would not submit passively to denigration any longer. "If
death is to be their portion, New Negroes are determined to make
their dying a costly investment for all concerned."[21] "The 'New
Crowd Negro' Making America Safe for Himself" described a concrete program necessary for black implementation immediately. The
first recommendation was "physical force in self-defense. While
force is to be deplored and used only as a last resort, it is indis-
pensable at times." A larger Negro police force and revolution were
the other two essential ingredients.[22]

Although Randolph and Owen often talked in dogmatic Socialist
terms, they also relied on good American sociologists such as Lester
Frank Ward for their analysis of the ills of our society. For example,
in a discussion of government ownership of the railroads, Randolph
noted that private profiteers would not give up their ownership of
property but "private ownership has been before the bar of public
opinion and found guilty. Historical evolution has decreed its fall."[23]
In frequent analyses, Randolph utilized Ward as his source of truth,
more often perhaps than Marx. The *Messenger* editors also prided
themselves upon their scientific and cool objectivity, in contrast,
they repeatedly said, to the approach of the old Negro leaders such
as DuBois. "The hope of the race," Owen claimed in one of his
many critiques of the black leaders, "rests in new leaders with a
more thorough grasp of scientific education, and a calm but uncompromising courage."[24]

Their analyses of the economic and social maladies rarely displayed a firm grasp upon reality. In one article by Randolph called
"The Negro Business Man," for example, the causes for his failure
sounded remarkably like the ones that Booker T. Washington also
recognized and tried to overcome. Randolph sagely counseled
Negro businessmen to unite, seek credit, and sell cheaply. "The
capital of Negroes in this country is enormous, but is not properly

---

[21] Editorial, "If We Must Die," *ibid.* (September, 1919): 4.

[22] Unsigned essay, "The 'New Crowd Negro' Making America Safe for Himself," *ibid.*, p. 21.

[23] Randolph, "The Negro Business Man," *ibid.* (January, 1918): 16.

[24] Chandler Owen, "The Failure of the Negro Leaders," *ibid.*, p. 24.

assembled, consequently, when the average colored man attempts to do business he is confronted with the absence of money—capital or the purchasing power with which to secure capital goods in which he proposes to deal."[25] Hardly a radical or imaginative explanation for the Negro businessman's troubles. In the area of politics, Randolph and Owen shared the general view that conditions were better in the North for blacks than in the South. In one editorial, southern migration was noted and the writer observed that Negroes were leaving the "land of the lynching bee and the home of the slave." In the North, "they secure better industrial opportunities, education for their children, and political power. From states in which they were disfranchised they go into states where they have a man's right to vote—the right to be freedmen in fact."[26]

From 1917 until around 1923, the *Messenger* strongly advocated the Socialist party as the only viable political party for black Americans. They criticized DuBois for his pragmatic advice to blacks to vote discreetly for local candidates of their choice and not to waste their votes upon the Socialist candidates, as they were sure losers. The International Workers of the World also received favorable mention from the *Messenger* in its early years. The IWW, they argued, was the only nondiscriminatory union, the only economic organization that did not bar blacks and appreciated the fact that the American struggle was on the basis of class and not color. Further, the Wobblies organized unskilled workers—a category in which most black workers fitted. Samuel Gompers and his American Federation of Labor received disapproving comments frequently. The exclusive craft unions systematically prevented blacks from entering their midst. A few AF of L unions that opened their doors to blacks obtained positive commendation. The Amalgamated Clothing Workers of America and the International Ladies Garment Workers, for example, were often praised for their union activities and the six-month strike of the ACW in the mid-twenties was enthusiastically supported.[27]

Nineteen twenty-three and twenty-four seemed to be a turning point for the *Messenger*. George Schuyler joined the staff and con-

---

[25] Randolph, "The Negro Business Man," *op. cit.*, p. 13.

[26] Editorial, "Migration and Political Power," *ibid.* 1 (July, 1918): 9.

[27] Note in the *Messenger*: "Reasons Why White and Black Workers Should Combine in Labor Unions," July, 1918, p. 14; "Why Negroes Should Join the IWW," July, 1919, p. 8; and "The Needle Trades Strikes," August, 1924.

tributed a witty, satirical column entitled "Shafts and Darts." A theater section, poetry, and numerous pictures became regular features of the previously staid polemical magazine. In discussing the 1924 presidential elections, Chandler Owen recommended to black voters to pull the lever for either Davis or La Follette so that the Republican party would realize that the Negro vote was no longer a sure thing. Randolph, in an article on the same subject a month later, suggested that La Follette was the most liberal and constructive candidate and deserved the Negro vote.[28] Both articles sounded very much like DuBois's political discussions of the previous ten years. Randolph and Owen, who had spent a great deal of their printing ink criticizing DuBois's pragmatism, now practiced it themselves. Madame Walker's beauty products were advertised in the *Messenger*, capitalism was extolled, and working within the party system seemed feasible.

In 1925, Randolph began organizing the Brotherhood of Sleeping Car Porters. The struggle to gain the support of the AF of L and to crush the giant Pullman Company was a long and arduous one. It would be another decade before victory came but Randolph's energies were now committed to the labor movement—not the IWW version but the AF of L model. The *Messenger* lost its radical tone and joined the *Crisis* and *Opportunity* in the mainstream of American black journalism.

While Randolph and Owen were independent Socialists, not card-carrying members of the Communist party, a small group of black Communists did exist in the twenties. In 1919, the Socialist party split and the Workers party of America became the organ for Moscow's programs. Randolph, as well as many other Socialists, refused to take orders from Moscow and continued to operate as autonomous Socialists who applied Marxian doctrine to the problems of American blacks. The African Blood Brotherhood, under Cyril Briggs, a light-skinned mulatto from the West Indies, became the mouthpiece for the Communists in the early twenties. However, in 1925 the brotherhood was replaced by the American Negro Labor Congress with Lovett Fort-Whiteman as its head. The goal of the congress, according to one report, was to convert the black worker

---

[28] Chandler Owen, "How the Negro Should Vote in This Campaign," *Messenger* 6 (September, 1924): 290–99; and A. Philip Randolph, "The Political Situation and the Negro," *ibid.* (October, 1924): 325–28, 330.

to bolshevism. "As Communists we hail this (Negro Labor) Congress as the beginning of a movement with far-reaching implications. Not merely can it

> be the means of starting to mobilize the Negro workers for a struggle against the degrading restrictions imposed upon them as a race, but as American workers speaking the common language of the country, they can become a power in the labor movement. Furthermore, they will receive training that will enable them to play an effective part in the world's mobilization of the oppressed colonial peoples against capitalism.[29]

The class analysis of the black man's problems in America was sure to create a counteranalysis. Abram Harris, for example, in an interesting report on the second annual American Negro Labor Congress, sympathetically surveyed the point of view of the black Communists. The Communist claim for social equality appealed to black Americans and the seeming brotherhood that existed within the congress impressed blacks who had heard DuBois and other black leaders preach social equality but to no avail. In the American Negro Labor Congress, black and white Communists worked together. (They did in the NAACP also, of course.) Further, the Communists' analysis argued that color prejudice was a plot of capitalists to turn the white proletariat away from their natural brothers. Harris considered this point the major weakness of the Communist position. Although economic deprivation surely played a major role in the black Americans troubles, the Marxist formula as a whole did not effectively describe the situation.

> They say that the Negro and white workers are members of the same economic class; their interests are identical, ergo, they will unite in proletarian solidarity against capitalism. But are the interests of white and black workers identical? If white and black workers will not unite in a trade union for economic self-preservation how much more unlikely is it that they will unite to promote the social revolution? . . . This much seems to me irrefuta-

---

[29] Quoted in "Bolshevizing the American Negro," *Independent,* 5 December 1925, p. 631.

ble: if their interests are identical there is little recognition of it on the part of white and black proletariat.[30]

Harris concluded that communism was the Garveyism of the middle 1920s. Its emotional appeal had the same impact on the masses with little material effect. The Marxist analysis, according to Harris, may have accurately described the causes of the proletariat's despair, but its attempts to deal with the race issue were singularly ineffective. Neither race thought strictly in economic terms; neither could transcend the color line. Surely, as DuBois and others frequently noted, white workers did not ally with black workers nor did they see their interests as identical.

To most of the Socialists, DuBois's radical credentials were marred because he supported the war effort and generally did not take a doctrinnaire line in his analysis of the race problem. Further, his rhetoric, though impassioned, rarely became excessive and inflammatory. A notable exception was his famous editorial of May, 1919, written to greet the returning black soldiers. In it, he reminded black people that this country was theirs, that they owed it to themselves and everyone else to work for its improvement, and that they should fight for the elimination of every evidence of prejudice and bias against black people. "This is the country to which we Soldiers of Democracy return"—a familiar theme, no doubt. But his passion became inflamed and he continued,

But by the God of Heaven, we are cowards and jackasses if now that that war is over, we do not marshal every ounce of our brain and brawn to fight a sterner, longer, more unbending battle against the forces of hell in our own land. *We return. We return from fighting. We return fighting.* Make way for Democracy! We saved it in France, and by the Great Jehovah, we will save it in the United States of America or know the reason why.[31]

This editorial was the exception, not the rule. DuBois, contrary to the editorial ravings of the *Crusader* and that ilk, was usually

---

[30] Abram L. Harris, Jr., "Lenin Casts His Shadow Upon Africa," *Crisis* 31 (April, 1926): 275.

[31] W. E. B. DuBois, "Returning Soldiers," *ibid.* 18 (May, 1919): 14.

temperate, rational, and analytical. He turned a fine phrase, coined good slogans, and generally wrote well. But the tone of his remarks rarely matched the emotional heights of the May, 1919, editorial. When discussing the Bolshevik Revolution, for example, he originally did not share the rapture of many American radicals. Claude McKay, the poet, in fact, criticized DuBois for his lukewarm discussion of the revolution. McKay, in a letter to DuBois, acknowledged the good work of the NAACP ("Your aim is to get for the American Negro the political and social rights that are his by virtue of the Constitution"[32]), but went on to point out the error of DuBois's view:

> But the Negro in politics and social life is ostracized only technically by the distinction of color; in reality the Negro is discriminated against because he is of the lowest type of worker.[33]

DuBois responded that although he had received much criticism for his support of the war and his seemingly cautious attitude toward the Russian Revolution, he did so out of his unswerving conviction "that the immediate work for the American Negro lies in America and not in Russia."[34] Further, a dogmatic commitment to Russian or German socialism would not solve the problems of American blacks. The white worker in America did not believe in the brotherhood of black workers. They systematically denied them entrance into their unions, ruthlessly used them as strikebreakers, and generally spewed hatred at all black workers. Thus, DuBois pleaded for a rational analysis and for a patient but determined commitment to the program of the NAACP.

In another article, DuBois forthrightly rejected revolution as a means of accomplishing the desired social changes.

> We do not believe in revolution. We expect revolutionary changes in many parts of this life and this world, but we expect these changes to come mainly through reason, human sympathy and the education of children, and not by murder. We know that

---

[32] Quoted in an editorial by DuBois, "The Negro and Radical Thought," *ibid.* 22 (July, 1921): 102.

[33] *Ibid.*

[34] *Ibid.*, p. 103.

there have been times when organized murder seemed the only way out of wrong, but we believe those times have been very few, the cost of the remedy excessive, the results as terrible as beneficent, and we gravely doubt if in the future there will be any real recurrent necessity for such upheaval.[35]

Again, DuBois pointed to the animosity that white workers felt for blacks and noted, in contrast, the increasing evidence that blacks were developing capital, buying and building in Harlem, and generally creating a black capitalistic class. "Whether this is a program of socialism or capitalism does not concern us. It is the only program that means salvation to the Negro race."[36] Time and time again DuBois pleaded for a rational discussion of the race problem and one that was founded upon empirical evidence. In still another discussion he commented that an idea did not have inherent validity because it was proposed by a worker while an idea created by a millionaire was inherently evil. "It must be judged by itself and not by its source."[37]

In 1926, however, DuBois visited the Soviet Union and wrote an enthusiastic account of his visit. "I stand in astonishment and wonder at the revelation of Russia that has come to me. I may be partially deceived and half-informed. But if what I have seen with my eyes and heard with my ears in Russia is Bolshevism, I am a Bolshevik."[38] First-hand observation convinced DuBois that the Bolsheviks had succeeded in organizing industry for public service[39] and, therefore, that they had accomplished their primary goal. In discussing black-white labor problems in 1928, DuBois also blamed white capitalists for inculcating prejudice into their white workers and turning them against their natural allies, the black workers.[40] Thus, he came closer to an orthodox Marxist explanation of the conflict between black and white workers. The white capitalists became the major enemy in this discussion; but the solution to the

---

[35] Editorial, "The Class Struggle," *ibid.* (August, 1921): 151.

[36] *Ibid.*, p. 152.

[37] W. E. B. DuBois, "Socialism and the Negro," *ibid.* (October, 1921): 246.

[38] W. E. B. DuBois, "Russia, 1926," *ibid.* 33 (November, 1926): 8.

[39] Undated letter from W. E. B. DuBois to Louis A. Carter, *ibid.* 34 (September, 1927): 240.

[40] W. E. B. DuBois, "Black and White Workers," *ibid.* 35 (March, 1928): 98.

problem still remained true to the pragmatic DuBois: disseminating the truth to both black and white labor groups through widely read and distributed periodicals. At the close of the decade of the twenties, then, DuBois may have used the vocabulary of Marxism, but his proposals were still very much within the typical American reform mold: better education, communication, and understanding through an effective press and school system.

Incidentally, there is an interesting parallel between the debate engaged in by the culture critics (Langston Hughes's argument for black cultural separatism versus George Schuyler's view of cultural sameness of blacks and whites) and the dialectic between the black reformers who remained within the American capitalistic scheme and the Communists. If the black American is part of a separate, peculiar race, then the class analysis of the doctrinnaire Communists would not obtain; class analysis, after all, crosses color, religious, and ethnic borders. On the other hand, if black Americans were merely dark-skinned whites, then a class analysis would be relevant. If black Americans, to explore a third possibility, were acceptors of the American value system, lovers of private property and material accumulation, then neither racist separatism nor communism would be particularly relevant or appropriate. The black intellectuals did not analyze these divergent views carefully or fully; often, they accepted, in good, eclectic, pragmatic American fashion, portions of each view. This was especially true when the black writers tried to encourage race pride at the same time that they espoused socialism. One way of reconciling this position, perhaps, could be the view that in a Socialist world, the brotherhood of man, with each particular race or ethnic group contributing its own rich uniqueness, would prevail.

Black writers of both the Harlem Renaissance school and the rural *Southern Workman* group often preached black pride while advocating American values of thrift, hard work, and individual effort. None of these people, as suggested in an earlier chapter, saw cultural autonomy or race pride as contrary to American ideals. Cultural pluralism, in the salad bowl of America, was the goal. Tolerance of differences, as long as the differences were cultural and religious and did not threaten the basic political and socioeconomic structures of American society, were quite acceptable. As long as labels were not attached to various schemes, they would be allowed. For example, DuBois's comment that he was not sure whether black economic activity could be defined as capitalism or socialism reflects a basically pragmatic American approach to a problem.

Rather than beginning with a theoretical premise, the American thinker and writer often begins with an analysis of the actual situation. He then tries to deal with it as rationally and fully as possible. So DuBois reckoned that autonomous economic power would aid the black man. The Marxists and Garveyites, in contrast, began with a comprehensive philosophy and then tried to change the people and circumstances to fit their theories. Marxism appeared as an alien philosophy for blacks in Harlem; further, it never fully appreciated the role and power of color prejudice in this country. Garveyism appealed to the emotions of black people but offered no viable program. There were no major concrete results from Garvey's views because they were untranslatable in America. Black Americans, even the West Indian emigrés, considered this country as their home and as the land of opportunity.

So far this chapter has argued that Garveyism and communism represented the two major bodies of thought that rejected the American Dream in the twenties. Their rhetoric as well as their goals seemed decidedly un-American. And yet there is a nagging and persistent possibility that the mystery and power of American values may have infected the radicals too. A. Philip Randolph at the end of the twenties was actively seeking the support of AF of L president William Green in his struggle to organize the Brotherhood of Sleeping Car Porters. Abram Harris noted as early as 1923 that "it is claimed in some circles that the *Messenger* editors have receded from their ultra-radical and Socialist position. Whether this be true or false, it is evident that the *Messenger* still sways the militant Left Wing."[41] And Frazier in 1928 commented:

> However, the *Messenger* is now no longer the spokesman of economic radicalism but has become an organ chiefly devoted to advertising Negro enterprises and boosting black capitalists. Such is the irony of fate![42]

Another way of approaching this intriguing possibility is to examine the evidence that congressional critics presented to convince

---

[41] Harris, "The Negro Problem as Viewed by Negro Leaders," *op. cit.*, p. 415.

[42] Frazier, *op. cit.*, p. 58.

themselves of the dangerous leftist nature of black radicals. Attorney General A. Mitchell Palmer included a discussion of "radicalism and sedition among Negroes" in his overall investigation for the Justice Department in 1919.[43] Similarly, a joint legislative committee in New York State in 1920, popularly called the Lusk Committee after its chairman, contained extensive examples of "Propaganda Among the Negroes."[44] Although they quoted profusely from the *Messenger*, a sampling of the more radical magazines is quite enlightening for our purposes. The *Crusader*, the organ of the African Blood Brotherhood, provided the investigators with seemingly scintillating reading:

> Just as by joining the IWW in large numbers we forced the AF of L to open its doors to us, so by joining the Socialist party we can force belated justice and consideration from the Republicans. . . .
> If to fight for one's rights is to be Bolshevist, then we are Bolshevists. . . . And for further information of the asses who use the term so loosely we will make the statement that we would not for a moment hesitate to ally ourselves with any group, if by such an alliance we could compass the liberation of our race. A man pressed to earth by another with murderous intent . . . would be a fool if he did not use any or whatever weapon was within his reach. Self-preservation is the first law of human nature.[45]

Perhaps it is the perspective of the 1970s, but these words do not appear to be particularly revolutionary. Surely the first quotation could as easily have been written for the *Crisis*. And the second one reflects basic self-interest, a motive no one would disagree with —abstractly stated. But most of the quoted material was from the war period, a period when emotions ran high and anyone who criticized the government's war aims or praised bolshevism, was immediately suspected as being a subversive. Issues of black and white radical magazines were confiscated in 1917 and 1918. *Chal-*

---

[43] Investigation Activities of the Department of Justice, 66th Cong., 1st sess., no. 153 (Washington: U.S. Government Printing Office, 1919). Hereafter cited as the *Palmer Report*.

[44] Report of the Joint Legislative Committee of the State of New York Investigating Seditious Activities, *Propaganda Among the Negroes*, vol. 2 (1920) chap. 5 (hereafter cited as the *Lusk Report*).

[45] *Palmer Report*, pp. 166–68.

lenge, edited by William Bridges, for example, had a shrill and extreme tone. It cried, "Negroes Unite! Brutal oppression is sweeping over like storm swept tidal waves,"[46] and elsewhere claimed,

> The South is more hellish than Germany ever was, even under its tyrannical regime of the Kaiser. The South in the twentieth century stoops to atrocities that only the South can stoop to without shame or remorse; from which Germany would recoil in loathing and disgust.[47]

These words confirmed every suspicion that Palmer and his cohorts had that, given the opportunity, black radicals would overthrow the American government.

Even the Lusk Committee, however, had to admit that black radicalism was founded upon white American injustice.

> One of the most important features of radical and revolutionary propaganda is the appeal made to those elements of our population that have a just cause of complaint with the treatment they have received in this country.[48]

And later in the report, they noted

> Much of this propaganda falls on fertile soil by reason of lynchings, Jim Crow legislation and the abridgement of the right of franchise to Negroes in many states.[49]

Thus, it could be argued, that the surprising fact of the period is the modest amount and extent of radical thought, writing, and activity. Given the blatantly unjust conditions under which black men had to live and work in America, the radicals should have been considerably more successful than they were. Their failure, I would submit, is inextricably tied to the fact that black Americans considered the American Dream their dream too. They rejected foreign interpretation or solution to their problems. They felt that the tools

---

[46] *Lusk Report,* pp. 1485–86.
[47] *Palmer Report,* pp. 168–71.
[48] *Lusk Report,* p. 1476.
[49] *Ibid.,* p. 1520.

and goals of America were sufficient to meet the needs of black Americans. Eventually, A. Philip Randolph and Chandler Owen also came to believe that the methods of America could accomplish the desired ends. And so they too returned to the American fold.

"If the American Negro becomes a radical it will be our fault, not Russia's."[50] So concluded an editorial in the conservative magazine the *Independent* in 1925. In the first thirty years of this century, disillusioned radical blacks, both of American and West Indian origin, may have rejected the hypocrisy of the American Dream and its false allure. Their rhetoric centered on either an international black movement or an international labor movement. In either case, they broke off the bonds of American nationalism and the individuality of the American culture. However, they did not find the overwhelming majority of black Americans responsive to their pleas. Garvey was the exception, not the rule. His appeal was based upon his own charismatic ability to sway his listeners. None of the black Communist spokesmen who followed Garvey into Harlem ever matched his membership. Black Americans appreciated the power of economics and the role it played in their lives. But they were interested in succeeding according to the American capitalistic standard. Black Americans responded to efforts to make them proud of their heritage but once again, they did not see this goal as incompatible with American values. The rejectors of the American Dream found that the constituency to which they appealed was, in fact, American, and did, in fact, adhere to the very dream that ignored them.

---

[50] Editorial, "Bolshevizing the American Negro," *op. cit.*, p. 631.

Chapter 7

1930

"The Negro must either get out, get white or get along."[1] It was very difficult in 1930 to do any of the things suggested in these words by Kelly Miller. "Between the middle of April and October, twenty-one lynchings were officially recorded, against ten for the entire twelve months of 1929. . . . When the illiterate whites below the Mason and Dixon line become desperate, it is time for the blacks to beware."[2] So observed one white southerner in the ominous year of 1930. However, to many black southerners, as George Schuyler wryly noted, the Depression did not make a tremendous impact because "the Negroes had been in the Depression all the time."[3] The economic catastrophe of late 1929 did not materially change the way of life, the mood, or the outlook of the majority of black Americans. It simply deepened the already dark reality.

Every man suffered but to black magazine writers, the harsh facts were not always apparent. Although *Opportunity*, the *Southern*

---

[1] Quoted in George S. Schuyler, "A Negro Looks Ahead," *American Mercury*, February, 1930, p. 212.

[2] Willie Snow Ethridge, "Salesmen of Violence," *Outlook*, 19 November 1930, p. 457.

[3] Quoted in Gilbert Osofsky, *Harlem: The Making of a Ghetto* (New York: Harper and Row, 1963), p. 149.

Workman, and the *Crisis* discussed the economic problems and hardships facing their brothers, their attitude, especially *Opportunity's* and the *Southern Workman's,* was sanguine. In an editorial in May, 1930, entitled "Jobs Without Labels," the editor of *Opportunity* noted the loss of Negro jobs but wondered whether it was not a blessing in disguise as it would eliminate wage differences and the permanent subservience of the Negro.

> Sure of a place on the lower occupational levels it has been easy for him to forego the rigorous training and bitter competition and racial prejudice to which he must submit himself if he attains the more highly skilled positions. As a result he has not fully developed that competitive spirit and the economic drive which are necessary if he shall survive in a competitive world.[4]

In retrospect, it appears incredulous that a black journal, aware of the gross discriminations facing black Americans, could suggest that the virtues of competitive capitalism needed to be learned by jobless blacks. Accepting the value of discipline and suffering, the editors suggested that survival of the fittest is the best possible course in this best of all possible worlds. The tone of *Opportunity* does not change in 1930; it remains rational, temperate, and cool. Its emotional level does not rise and its sense of urgency or emergency does not increase.

The *Southern Workman* reflected the same placid demeanor. Although located in the South, where the number of black landowners (however small their holdings) had dropped sharply and the number of sharecroppers had risen from 39 percent in 1920 to 46 percent in 1925,[5] the *Southern Workman* featured exotic articles on African tribal cultures, individual black American success stories, and inspirational commencement addresses. While millions of acres of farm land had been taken out of cultivation and was becoming "broomsage and brambles,"[6] the *Southern Workman* published reports about a unique and exceptional truck farmer in Montgomery, Alabama, who used modern equipment.[7]

---

[4] Editorial, "Jobs Without Labels," *Opportunity,* May, 1930, p. 135.

[5] Ruth G. Bergman, "The Negro's Livelihood," *Survey,* 15 October 1930, pp. 80–81.

[6] *Ibid.,* p. 81.

[7] See J. T. Alexander, "Negro Farmer Operates Modern Truck Farm," *Southern Workman* 59 (February, 1930): 71–73.

In the rare articles that dealt with the bleak southern reality, the solutions proposed were frequently rhetorical and platitudinous. For example, William Holtzclaw, the principal of the Utica Normal and Industrial Institute in Mississippi, wrote on the "Present Status of the Negro Farmer in Mississippi."[8] After noting that overproduction caused lower prices, thereby hurting Negro cotton farmers, he advised his readers to "go up and possess the land."[9] After mildly criticizing the Federal Land Bank for its preferential treatment of plantation owners, he weakly noted that the plantation system was breaking down, thus implying that the federal bank would reverse its policies and favor the poor, insecure black farmer. He concluded with a praiseworthy comment on the Mississippi farmer: "He is a poorly trained, hard working, constantly praying, God-fearing Christian citizen."[10]

George Ketcham, the field secretary of Hampton Institute, gave a radiobroadcast speech on the American Negro from London in June of 1930. The speech, reprinted in the *Southern Workman,* provided Englishmen with a cautiously optimistic estimate of the black man's status in America. "The manner in which the Negro is entering industry is shown by the fact that out of 321 occupations listed in New York City there were only nine in which it was found recently that there were no Negroes."[11] No mention, of course, is made as to whether the relative percentage for black Americans in each respective category is equitable. Did black Americans, representing one-tenth of the population, have anywhere near their share of doctors, lawyers, engineers, and advertising executives? Ketcham commented on the poor record of the labor unions in admitting blacks but ended with ". . . a favorable change is occurring."[12] Radio listeners in London who used Ketcham's description as the basis for their view of Negro Americans had a distorted vision indeed.

The Horatio Alger model also continued to receive attention in the pages of the *Southern Workman* in the unlikely year of 1930. "Plastering A Way Through"[13] must stand as a superb example of

---

[8] William Holtzclaw, "Present Status of the Negro Farmer in Mississippi," *ibid.* (August, 1930): 339–44.

[9] *Ibid.*, p. 344.

[10] *Ibid.*

[11] George F. Ketcham, "A Brief View of the American Negro," *ibid.* (October, 1930): 471.

[12] *Ibid.*

[13] Allen B. Daggett, Jr., "Plastering A Way Through," *ibid.*, pp. 449–53.

American know-how, devotion to WASP values, and undying faith in a system even when the reality defied its eternal validity. William Brown of Philadelphia was a successful plasterer—the largest Negro contractor in the city, no less. His payroll ran between $3500 and $4000 a week and although he was not a union member, he paid union wages. Brown believed that Philadelphia was an open city. His life seemed to be a living example of what results from hard work and Christian values. Thus, the *Southern Workman* did not change or vary its fare in 1930. The same outlook, the same philosophy continued to motivate its editors and writers. Whether the poor delta farmers in Mississippi shared the magazine's optimism is hard to say, but a fair guess would be that they did not.

When James E. Piggott, a prominent Louisiana planter, pleaded guilty of holding Negro farm hands in peonage in 1930, he replied: "I handled niggers in the way every other planter handles them."[14] Peonage, rather than widescale individual success in the city or on the farm, was the reality for many southern black farmers. Nineteen thirty was a drought year and this natural horror only accentuated the grim fate of marginal agricultural workers barely eking a living out of an unsympathetic land. Convict leasing, sharecropping, and tenant farming were merely twentieth-century methods of enslavement. When Negroes left the land for the promised land of the big city, they found conditions equally inhospitable. During the Depression, Atlanta fired all blacks in the sanitary department and whites became the street sweepers and garbage collectors.[15] Things were no better in northern cities. In Chicago, for example, by 1935 when 13.7 percent of all Chicago families were on welfare, 46 percent of all Negro families were receiving relief.

What could be done? What course remained open to blacks? George Schuyler, the satirist-journalist, provided a thoughtful discussion of this subject in an article for *American Mercury*, a magazine, incidentally, which published much of his writing. "A Negro Looks Ahead"[16] analyzed the various options open to black Americans: emigration, miscegenation, separatism, accommodation. Schuyler rejected the first three alternatives as unrealistic solutions

---

[14] Walter Wilson, "Cotton Peonage," *New Republic,* 16 December 1931, p. 131.

[15] Bergman, *op. cit.,* p. 82.

[16] Schuyler, *op. cit.,* pp. 212–20.

and settled upon the last one as the only possible course of action. He appeared, however, to come to this answer reluctantly and only after reviewing quite carefully the other alternatives. For example, Schuyler analyzed statistics on black capitalism provided by Abram Harris and the National Negro Business League to determine the efficacy of black separatism and concluded that most black business was in the ghetto and largely devoted to personal services. Further, black businessmen did not employ sufficient black workers to become a meaningful capitalistic unit. This evidence, coupled with his implicit assumption that blacks were Americans, convinced him that revolution was improbable, exportation unrealistic, and intermingling unlikely in the short run. Thus, blacks had to devise methods of adjusting and accommodating themselves to the white man's world if they were to survive and succeed.

The white popular magazines' treatment of the black man did not improve during the Depression. In the few cases where blacks were discussed, the tone and the solution remained factual, and did not depict any kind of extraordinary problem. One article in the *Nation*, for example, deplored the War Department's policy of segregating the widows and mothers of black soldiers who were going to France to visit their boys' graves. Fifty-five black women cancelled their reservations because of this policy. "The government must learn," editorialized the *Nation*, "that the Negroes are no longer property to be shunted around back alleys and smuggled in at side doors. They are American citizens with a vote."[17] How was the government to learn this lesson? Who was prepared or able to teach it to Mr. Hoover in 1930? Or to Congress? Or to the courts? The rhetoric sounded empty but, after all, the *Nation* has to be credited with raising their voice on a subject that received virtually no attention in official circles.

In contrast to the blandness of the *Southern Workman* and the lack of bite in *Opportunity*'s commentary on the Depression, the *Crisis* offered more articles and more discussions of the economic catastrophe and how it affected blacks. Abram Harris, a rising black economist of the period, contributed one article on "The Negro Worker: A Problem of Progressive Labor Action,"[18] in which he

---

[17] Editorial, "Black and Gold Stars," *Nation*, 23 July 1930, pp. 85–86.

[18] Abram L. Harris, "The Negro Worker: A Problem of Progressive Labor Action," *Crisis*, March, 1930, pp. 83–85.

recommended the formation of a labor party as well as the creation of an effective trade union organization. The advocacy of a political party based upon an economic class was reminiscent of Tom Watson's Populist party hopes in the 1890s. Clearly, such an idea was not a customary or popular one in America. The two-party system, composed of a polygot of interests, deemphasized, if not denied, any class description of themselves. Harris contended that black and white workers, sharing the same economic fate, could and would unite in a common political party as well as a common labor union if their mutual interest was pointed out to them. He saw this end as the only solution to the terrible economic fate of blacks. It is interesting to read this view from Harris as only a short while before he had been critical of the Communist party for its naïve belief that it could organize black and white workers together. The white workers' stubborn lack of recognition of a common interest with blacks, largely motivated by emotional race prejudice, made a political and economic alliance highly unlikely. The Depression, however, which only dramatized the black's economic vulnerability, seemed to make Harris forget his doubts and revitalize the *hope* of an economic union of both races.

DuBois spoke frequently of cooperatives as a viable method available to blacks for their economic betterment. If blacks collectivized their resources, pooled their capital, and shared their talents, they could buy more cheaply and effectively. The boycott was also discussed as an effective measure available to discerning black buyers. A quotation from the Chicago *Whip*, for example, reported on a successful boycott of South Side Chicago businesses that did not hire black employees.[19] Woolworth's in Chicago was also boycotted. DuBois suggested in one discussion of the telephone company's unwillingness to hire blacks that they should not vote in franchises for this quasi-public institution. "Government ownership is the only solution for this present industrial disfranchisement of the Negro."[20] Elsewhere, DuBois quoted George Schuyler who noted that nice white philanthropists should go beyond giving money to black schools and begin allowing blacks to work in their factories.[21]

The solutions proposed by DuBois and other writers in the *Crisis*

---

[19] DuBois, "Postscript: Our Economic Peril," *Crisis*, March, 1930, pp. 101–2.

[20] DuBois, "Postscript: Economic Disfranchisement," *ibid.*, August, 1930, p. 281; and DuBois, "Postscript: Jobs," *ibid.*, November, 1930, p. 389.

[21] DuBois, "Postscript: Our Economic Peril," *op. cit.*, p. 101.

may not have been realistic or possible, but compared with the apathetic attitude or modest treatment the subject received in the other journals, *Crisis* must be credited with a keen awareness and desperate interest in designing solutions to this complex and mammoth problem. In one particularly interesting discussion of the differences and similarities between the NAACP and the Communist-backed American Negro Labor Congress, DuBois displayed his fervent commitment to American methods and goals despite the harsh economic reality.

> The Labor Congress lays its chief emphasis on the organization of labor and criticizes the NAACP as the potential leader of a class of small capitalists in opposition to the interests of the laborers.[22]

DuBois, quite sensitive to this charge, heatedly rejected it as a totally inaccurate picture of the NAACP's work. His organization, he countered, had never sided with the capitalists against the workers. But living in America demanded a delicate and difficult understanding of its unique problems:

> We live in the greatest capitalistic country of the age and probably of all ages. We must look that fact square in the face and endeavor, in the first place, to align ourselves with those who seek to correct the evils of capitalistic organization, and, at the same time, preserve its tremendous possibilities for good. This is a hard road. In countries, like Russia, it has led to war and revolution; and our chief difference with the American Negro Labor Congress is that we do not believe that similar reform in the United States need entail violence. It will call for sacrifice, patience, clear thinking, determined agitation, and intelligent voting. But if civilization is not a failure, it will call for nothing more than this. And on this platform the NAACP puts its feet.[23]

This statement seems important for a number of reasons. First, it demonstrates DuBois's essential devotion to the validity of the American Dream and its effective implementation for black Americans in the bleak year of 1930. Second, it shows his dogged belief

---

[22] W. E. B. DuBois, "Postscript: Programs of Emancipation," *ibid.*, April, 1930, p. 137.

[23] *Ibid.*

in nonviolent, legalistic, and legislative solutions to the race problem in America. Thirdly, DuBois's rejection of a dogmatic class analysis of this society reveals his flexible, pragmatic use of Marx and his unwillingness to identify with a Soviet solution to an American problem. One crucial qualifier, however, appears in this statement: "but if civilization is not a failure, it will call for nothing more than this." But what if civilization (namely, white Anglo-Saxon Protestant culture) is a failure? What if the white establishment does not respond to clear thinking, determined agitation, and intelligent voting? How long must one wait to decide if civilization has failed or not? DuBois does not confront this chilling supposition in this article. The decade of the thirties made him reevaluate his commitment to Americanism. But in 1930 DuBois still tried desperately to adapt American capitalism to the needs of black Americans.

In the December issue, DuBois disputed Hoover's view that the Depression was temporary and that there was no fundamental wrong in our society. DuBois identified the deep wrong as being the lack of a social ethic to control economic activity. Not until moral concerns governed businessmen and exploitation for the profit motive was eliminated would American capitalism be made humanly fruitful and desirable.[24] There was plenty of food in America, DuBois noted, but it was not being distributed because of the profit motive. This attitude had to be overcome. Thus, DuBois hoped that capitalism could be humanized, that the needs of people could receive priority over the demand for profit. Whether this could (or can) be achieved remains a critical question.

Simultaneous with the discussions of the economic crisis, DuBois discussed political accomplishments and activities as well. The most notable success in 1930 was the Senate's refusal to confirm the nomination of the southern racist Judge Parker to the Supreme Court. DuBois advised his readers to vote against those senators who supported Parker and claimed, at the end of the year, that black voters had contributed significantly to the defeat of Allen of Kansas and McClulloch of Ohio, two pro-Parker senators.[25] Thus, political participation continued to be discussed as a meaningful and desirable tool in the struggle for black equality. Typical of all years of this

---

[24] DuBois, "Fundamentals," *ibid.*, December, 1930, p. 426.
[25] DuBois, "The Elections," *ibid.*, p. 425.

century, the events represented mixed results in the battle to eliminate race discrimination. William Pickens's "Re-Visiting the South" reported that "the great outstanding phenomenon is the 'stand-pat' condition of the South on race relations." Further, he noted that "if anything dethrones Jim Crow, it will be economic causation combined with the enforcement of constitutional law."[26]

A victory in the Parker case did not, and could not, offset the Depression and the dogged determination of the South to stand still. While black northerners could obtain some modest relief aid to modify the harsh reality of unemployment and starvation, the black southerner did not even have this minimal assistance. White southerners, conditioned by years of practice, offered the meager funds available to poor whites and not to blacks. Further, before the New Deal programs, whatever aid given was on the state and local level. Given the South's low taxing and public service tradition, the results did not portend well for blacks. Even when New Deal relief programs were instituted, white southern administrators discriminated against needy blacks. "Civil and political rights for them," said A. Philip Randolph, "are virtually unknown. . . . Relief, though given by the Federal Government, is administered by whim of southern prejudice in the mood of arrogant superiority."[27] Thus, blacks received substantially less relief payment than poor whites. Because blacks were largely unskilled city workers or marginal farm workers, they were laid off first, obtained little or no governmental welfare assistance, and thus faced the thirties with dim prospects of better days ahead.

In one textbook discussion of wages in the South for textile workers, it was noted that Negro females received the lowest pay with Negro males and white women next.

In general, the Negro suffered a differential of from 20 to 30 percent, and the white women slightly less. This latter was one of the factors leading to widespread female employment in southern textile and tobacco industries.[28]

---

[26] William Pickens, "Re-Visiting the South," *ibid.*, April, 1930, p. 127.

[27] Quoted in Thomas C. Cochran, *The Great Depression and World War II* (Chicago: Scott, Foresman, 1968), p. 105.

[28] Thomas D. Clark and Albert D. Kirwan, *The South Since Appomattox* (New York: Oxford University Press, 1967), p. 231.

The disease of bigotry pervaded all of southern society. There was no escaping it. Human labor was cheap, tractors were viewed, as late as 1930, as exotic, newfangled inventions, and black labor was especially available and expendable. Malnutrition, a high infant mortality rate, miserable living conditions, and marginal survival characterized the life of southern blacks. As Langston Hughes said: "The Depression brought everything down a peg or two, and the Negro had but few pegs to fall."[29]

While northern black communities tried to organize "Don't buy where you can't work" campaigns (with the black magazines and leaders providing support), southern blacks had neither the leadership, the resources, nor the energy to initiate self-help projects. Nineteen thirty was a bad year for black men in all sections of the country, but clearly the Southland won the prize for the worst place for blacks to live. Once again, then, the black intellectual view that life in the North was materially better than life in the South proved true. Political power may have been modest, economic might may not have succeeded in getting job equality for blacks, and social equality was still in the future, but the prospects for all of these goals being achieved seemed feasible in the North. The dream had viability in the North in 1930, despite the hardships and terrible conditions. In the South, it must have been a mockery.

The view obtained from the black magazines suggests no weakening of the commitment to the American Dream. The Depression, after all, was not a conspiracy against blacks but a serious collapse affecting white Americans as well. Communists did not receive significant numbers of converts from either the black or white community. DuBois and his readers still believed that the NAACP, and not the National Negro Labor Congress, provided the only meaningful path to salvation. Faith in the ultimate workability of the system was not materially shaken. Although DuBois, Randolph, and others were convinced that capitalism needed serious restructuring, they still thought constructive changes could be achieved through legislative, lobbying, and propaganda techniques. They did not advocate or consider a violent revolution as desirable or necessary. Perhaps their unwillingness to consider violence as desirable made them conclude that it was also unnecessary. In any case, their devo-

---

[29] Osofsky, *op. cit.*, p. 187.

tion to the possibility of change, of progress within the system, seemed intact.

While *Opportunity's* editors still praised the virtues of competition, and recommended to their readers that they take the virtues of competition to heart, DuBois preached the need for cooperation and the softening of the profit motive as the major *raison d'etre*. This fundamental difference of opinion clearly represented a major break in the ideological sphere between DuBois and the Urban League leadership. It may also characterize the beginning of the split that occurred in 1934 between DuBois and the NAACP leadership. As DuBois moved farther and farther away from accepting the basic premise of capitalism, and became more and more convinced that it could not reform itself, his enchantment with the American Dream disappeared. This occurred, of course, after more than thirty years of involvement and energetic engagement within the confines of the system.

The American Dream, however, did not die. It endured despite the bleak reality; the overwhelming majority of black intellectuals became New Dealers in the the thirties. A. Philip Randolph and Chandler Owen, rebels of the twenties, for example, became active supporters of the trade union movement and the New Deal. Although they had their quarrels with FDR in the thirties, they still believed that significant concessions could be obtained for black Americans within the political and economic structures of America. The Urban League and the NAACP continued their efforts at chipping away at the legal violations, the injustices, and the institutional forms of discrimination against black Americans.

Nineteen thirty did not mark a sudden break with the past. Despite the catastrophic depression of the previous year, black leaders did not dramatically alter their vision of America or their methodology. Their strategy remained the same although the problems deepened and became dramatic. The power of the American Dream myth, with its absolute commitment to positive change and to inevitable progress beguiled black intellectuals into believing that the Depression would be overcome, the status and material conditions of black America would be significantly ameliorated, and that white America would right her past wrongs to her black compatriots. The empirical evidence to support this faith was not forthcoming; neither was it necessary as it was a faith.

Chapter 8

A Final View

One of the persistent questions that arises from this discussion is: How responsive, in fact, is the American system to criticism? According to the dream myth, mobility, change, and the willingness to change are inherent characteristics of America. However, the blatant and consistent unwillingness of the various institutions in this country to deal honestly and respectfully with the race problem suggests an opposite conclusion. Neither the national legislature, the judicial system, nor the executive provided adequate responses during the first third of this century. And yet, as has been abundantly demonstrated, the black writers never gave up hope (with the exception of the group discussed in Chapter 6) and continued to operate within the American value system.

Black commentators who considered the Marxian analysis and solution desirable and applicable to this country often stopped short of advocating revolution as the only possible way of obtaining the wanted result. They too believed implicitly in the flexibility of the American system. DuBois, for example, in one discussion of black and white workers accepted the Marxian view that the white capitalist is the chief exploiter of both labor groups. He went on to say that black workers have to be educated to understand that they should not be scabs while white workers must be educated to realize the commonality of interests they share with the blacks. How can this education (the first step toward social change) be accomplished? DuBois suggested that periodicals, widely disseminated, must provide the truth to both black and white workers.[1] This solution to the mammoth problem just described seems almost ludicrous. But it effectively demonstrates the tremendous power the American Dream has upon its citizenry, even its educated and articulate critics. Further, even when the critic's analysis is in "un-American" terms, his solution is very much within the American framework.

The indomitable spirit of men like DuBois cannot fail to impress anyone who reads the literature of 1900–1930. This point cannot be overstressed. Note one additional example of this. In a discussion of the fight for equal rights in America in 1921, DuBois states:

Far from being discouraged in the fight, we are daily more and more triumphant. Yesterday, 1,650 Negro women voted in New Orleans. Never since 1876 have so many Negroes voted in the South as in the last election. Our fight for right has the enemy on the run. He has had to retreat to mob violence, secret and silly mummery, clumsy and hypocritical promises. Twenty-five years more of the intelligent fighting that the NAACP has led will make the black man in the United States free and equal.[2]

Granted the propaganda and rallying cry nature of these remarks. Granted that DuBois was hoping for a self-fulfilling prophesy—if you say it is so, it will be so—but nevertheless, it demonstrates his implicit commitment to progress and the triumph of truth in the eternal battle against evil forces. As already suggested, however, this faith began to wear out after 1930.

Black critics, in order to boost their argument, could point to historical precedents in which America demonstrated her responsiveness to the demands of minorities. The Populists, although eventually co-opted by the Democrats, had some of their demands met. They lost their original purity as well as their comprehensive program and goals, but they obtained something in return. This,

---

[1] W. E. B. DuBois, "Black and White Workers," *Crisis* 35 (March, 1928): 98.

[2] W. E. B. DuBois, "The Drive," *ibid.* 22 (May, 1921): 8.

too, is an accepted part of the compromise nature of America's political system. There is a price for responsiveness; and it is accommodation. DuBois certainly appreciated this and was more than willing to pay the price. In an interesting reply to the writer Margaret Deland's request that he criticize the election of Oscar DePriest to Congress because of the latter's alleged ineptitudes and corrupt connections, DuBois reminded Miss Deland that Congressman DePriest supported the enforcement of the Thirteenth, Fourteenth, and Fifteenth Amendments, the passage of the Dyer Anti-Lynching Bill, abolition of Jim Crow cars in interstate commerce, and the ending of color segregation in the civil service of the United States. He went on to say that he wished DePriest was against big business and corruption but

> We find ourselves compelled in political life, therefore, to choose the least of evils. If we remember that Senator Borah stands for clean politics, we also are compelled to remember that he stands for the disfranchisement of Negroes; that he did not vote for the Dyer Anti-Lynching Bill, and that he has grown dumb in the fight for Haiti.

DuBois concluded this discussion by indicating that the fight for democracy in America is more important "than prohibition, crime and privilege. Given democracy in this land and we can fight drunkenness, prostitution and monopoly; without democracy and with a 'Solid South' we can only wobble between Hoover and Raskob."[3]

Compromise was not a curse, especially in the political arena. Black commentators appreciated the necessity to work within a system that recognized that perfection was unattainable. The black critics surely knew that life was imperfect; they simply wanted to lessen the grossest examples of injustice and discrimination. They were not utopians. By giving black men their rights, the ultimate brotherhood of man would not occur automatically. But the demands were great and the needs were pressing. Certain goals, of course, such as voting rights, the end of violence, educational opportunity, and job equality were not negotiable. DuBois would have preferred to talk in terms of socialism, and of comprehensive changes in the economic structure of society, but he shrewdly knew

---

[3] W. E. B. DuBois, "Postscript," *ibid.* 36 (February, 1929): 57.

that the word socialism elicited negative emotional responses from most black and white Americans; so he contented himself with specific, seemingly undebatable civil rights demands. But what appeared to DuBois to be an obviously just goal seemed otherwise to most white Americans.

Thus, even the nature of compromise, or rather its possibility, was severely lessened because white Americans would not even entertain the most modest proposals. Thus, what could you negotiate? Seen from this perspective, the American system, indeed, was unresponsive to black demands. There were no crumbs to be negotiated. Each civil rights goal contained substance and each one, if implemented, would have changed the political, social, and economic relationships of black and white people. The myth of flexibility remained a myth. Token changes could not be allowed because none of the desired reforms were tokens. Political compromise could not be utilized to deal effectively with the problem. In the few instances in this country where it was called forth, most notably in Chicago and Harlem, the successful control of the black candidate and voter by the dominant white party made the black man's participation in politics an empty victory. But, as DuBois suggested, every step toward black political involvement was a step forward. Knowing the price of success, black advocates of political compromise still believed it was well worth paying.

Chastising the South became a favorite theme of many black writers during this period. The South surely was the bane of existence for many of the civil rights advocates. The gross examples of racism, the blatant disfranchisement of black citizens, and the resulting political power the South wielded in the Congress of the United States made that region's sins appear more significant as well as more widespread than the developing discrimination and racism in the new urban ghettoes of the North. In reality, however, during the years 1900–1922 there was an average of one race riot every year *with the number evenly divided between the North and the South.* Yet the perception of most black and white commentators was that the situation was far worse in the South than in the North. The lynchings and open racism surely contributed to this view as did the pragmatic understanding that whatever significant white support the NAACP or Urban League had was in the North. It was certainly easier to focus upon the evils of the South. Thus, DuBois for one, spent a great deal of time discussing both the constructive and the destructive activities that occurred in the South. Every southern election was carefully described and analyzed with on the spot reports from Walter White and others. The North did not go unnoticed. Walter White also wrote about residential segregation in Detroit and the famous Sweet trial for the *Crisis*. But the bulk of criticism, especially when discussing politics, was aimed at the South. Editorials and articles, however, printed in *Crisis*, could not change the political structure of the South. The means at the disposal of black critics were inadequate to deal with the problem. Only the federal government, through vigorous enforcement of its laws, could solve the dilemma. The courts did not effectively challenge the right of each state to determine its voting procedures and qualifications, and during this period, the administrations of Harding, Coolidge, and Hoover were not disposed to do so either.

The South's estimate of the race problem showed itself to be the most realistic and accurate. In this century, the true meaning of black emancipation has become evident; it is nothing short of a social revolution. This was precisely the fear of southerners since the days of slavery. The northern unwillingness to consider the tremendous implications of abolishing slavery must be viewed as a contribution to the problem. When black southerners began migrating in large numbers to northern cities and race riots soon followed, white southerners shook their heads knowingly. The North found itself in a terrible dilemma; for years they had repudiated the Ku Klux Klan, racism, and discriminatory treatment of black citizens. Now their choice was either to renounce their past words and join the South in stamping out blacks or to live up to their own pronouncements. The luxury of fine sentiments was now going to be tested.

Essentially, the North took neither of these courses. They created a third: equivocal reiteration of the beautiful American rhetoric at the same time that blacks were systematically denied jobs, good housing, and educational equality. Thus, the North worked out its own, hypocritical solution to the race problem. They would continue to mouth the ideals of America while they practiced the reverse of it. The South rightly condemned the North for hypocrisy. The terrible tragedy, of course, was that nowhere in this country did anyone try to live according to American principles.

Thus, the mythic elasticity and openness of the American system was nonexistent in the North and the South. This is not to say that

American institutions were inherently unable to fulfill the rhetoric of America, but rather that the leaders within each of the respective regions and institutions chose not to do so. They chose to interpret the American Dream as being the monopoly of white Americans; the promise of America did not apply to black Americans. As long as the structures of America continued to exist, though, there would be critics who would point out the hypocrisy and the gap that existed between the potential and the real. In every society, there is always some distance between what the society's ideals are and what the reality is. However, when the gap widens, rather than narrows, it is certainly a sign of malfunctioning. Further, when the society provides the avenues and the agencies to seek redress, to bridge the gap, but fails to allow some groups access to these agencies, then a serious schism is inevitable. This unbridgeable gap, if you will, began during the first thirty years of this century and continues to broaden to this day.

Another concern that emerges from this discussion is the dilemma of the black literary artists. The core of identity of any artist is his artistic merit. His self-definition, often dependent upon the view of others as well, is based on his demonstrated talent. Thus, a black writer, like any other writer, must believe that his imaginative work is worthy of concern, exciting, and exceptional. Some artists who have a very strong personal sense do not need the approval of others; but most artists, as most people, require some external approval of their efforts to confirm their judgment. Harlem, by the mid-twenties, provided a cohesive community of talented, articulate black writers who could share ideas, interact, and criticize each others' work. The Harlem Renaissance, more than being an outpouring of many great literary pieces, was the first time in black American history that a significant number of free and educated blacks could live and work together creatively and could earn a living by their labor.

Black writers found themselves confounded by the very same dangers that faced all writers. The danger of pandering to public taste, of lowering their artistic standards in order to succeed, plagued black writers as well as white writers. The danger of being daring for the sake of daring also existed. But in addition to these concerns, black writers had to face their blackness and their relationship to their black brothers. Should their writing only deal with race themes? Could, or should, they write colorless prose? According to Wallace Thurman, the color blindness of Countee Cullen and his slavish devotion to white conventions made his poetry banal and insipid. It was only when black writers captured the uniqueness of black people at the same time that they expressed their art in universal terms, Thurman argued, that great literature was produced. This formula was difficult to achieve. Indeed, it is difficult for any writer, regardless of color, to portray the particular and the abstract simultaneously. Great literature is hard to come by in any group.

V. F. Calverton, the noted white radical literary critic, commented in an analysis of black art and literature in 1929 that the new crop of black writers were less sentimental, more forthright, and more daring in their fiction and poetry than their black predecessors. He compared James David Corrothers unfavorably to Claude McKay and Langston Hughes and suggested that Corrothers's writing was too meek and submissive in contrast to McKay's open defiance of the white man's feelings. In the 1920s, the black poets could say: "If we must die—let it not be like hogs," while Corrothers had said a few years earlier, "To be a Negro in a day like this—/Alas! Lord God, what ill have we done?" Assertiveness had succeeded acquiescence. Further, Calverton noted the new interest in proletarian heroes in black fiction in contrast to the middle- and professional-class heroes in the fiction of Jessie Fauset and Walter White. Calverton pointed to Rudolph Fisher's and Claude McKay's writings as examples of lower-class life and heroes being depicted.[4]

This trend, of course, is typical of the general direction that literature has taken; first a concern with upper-class life and protagonists and then a concern for the lower classes. It demonstrated the black writer's self-confidence and willingness to show the white world all levels of black society, but it also showed the traditional Western fascination with lower-class life and the romanticizing of poverty. Realistic fiction is often viewed as evidence of a maturation point in a peoples' fictional development. By 1930, black writing contained examples of both sentimental and realistic fiction, but neither genre overtook the other. The two coexisted. For the purposes of

---

[4] V. F. Calverton, "The New Negro's New Belligerent Attitude," *Current History* 30 (September, 1929): 1081–88.

our central theme, the American Dream and its failure continued to be a vital one, whether portrayed from the point of view of a black doctor or a stevedore.

Finally, the concept of cultural pluralism received much attention in the black writings of this particular period. Whether we look at the agriculturally oriented *Southern Workman* or the urban *Crisis,* we see examples of black writers defining the areas of human life in which black autonomy could be preserved without doing violence to American ideals. While white Americans provided the models for political and economic success, black people and their unique experiences became the source for religion, a new education, and a revitalized cultural life. Black music, art, and singing did not, and did not have to, borrow from white culture. Black religion contained its own spiritual and irreplaceable qualities; and black education, emphasizing the black man's history and contribution to American life (a part of his education which white men conspicuously ignored), would produce psychologically whole black children who took pride in their blackness and in their people's past. The Harlem Renaissance, as well as Hampton Institute, attempted to create cultural separatism *within* the American organism—a separatism which would not destroy the essential wholeness of America.

A study could easily be done regarding the American myth of tolerance and respect for difference. This view seems to be implicitly contained in the larger American Dream myth. However, it seems to be the least articulated as well as the least practiced part of the dream mythology. The overriding interest in conformity obliterates respect for differences. Thus, black assertiveness of their different past and their separate traditions would surely bring belligerent and antagonistic responses from white Americans. Difference in America has generally been defined to mean superiority. Whether the articulators of separatism say it or not is irrelevant. The perceivers deem it to be an aloof and undemocratic manner to adopt in egalitarian America. In order to prove American equality, everyone must look and act alike. From 1900 to 1930, black Americans did not proclaim loudly and publicly their cultural difference from white Americans. Most black spokesmen, as has been abundantly demonstrated, argued the sameness of blacks with whites and denied any differences. White Americans should give black

Americans their equal rights precisely because they too were human beings, citizens of the same country, and practitioners of American values.

The small minority of blacks in Harlem who waxed eloquent on the theme of black culture did not reach a major audience. The writers of the *Southern Workman* did not couch their urgings in radical or threatening language. Neither did they say anything that sounded other than commonsensical. But the implications of their views, the logical culmination of cultural pluralism, requires a healthy respect for different points of view and different styles of living. America developed the myth of the melting pot because she could not tolerate differences. Similarly, she would not countenance groups within her midst who suggested other than the accepted middle-class cultural goals. The implications of this dilemma, however, were not realized for another thirty years. Meanwhile, black culture advocates propagandized for their black brothers to abandon the white man's standards and replace it with their own. But for every Langston Hughes, there were innumerable George Schuylers who scoffed at the idea of a separate and authentic black culture. American goals, for good or ill, were shared by black Americans equally with white Americans.

Cultural pluralism was not effectively realized in the 1920s. As a principle, it still has not won wide adherence. Many ethnic groups have preserved their ties with a religion and culture imported from Europe, but they practice their ethnicity privately. They do not make a public display of it. Cultural pluralism is secretly and discreetly practiced by a few but frowned upon by the majority as un-American. Black Americans found themselves in the equivocal position of being neither Americans nor black people. The demonstrated benefits of white American society were denied them and their black African cultural heritage was too remote to recapture. The ordinary black person experienced his religion and culture and knew it to be different from white people. But he could easily merge this culture with Americanism—or with the hope of eventual entry into the democratic opportunities this country promised her citizens. Black intellectuals, on the other hand, could entertain the belief that the African past could be revitalized and amalgamated or brought into parallel operation with the American culture. They saw the African past as an integral part of the black man's experience in twentieth-century America while the ordinary black man's sense of his difference was largely based upon his deprived status.

While the black intellectual romanticized the African past, the illiterate black remembered slavery and his continued subjugation since emancipation.

Black intellectuals were not talking to the black masses. They were talking to each other. Their theoretical discussions of cultural pluralism did not reach the real life situations of most black people in America. But their gropings for a genuine synthesis of blackness into white American culture, with the black ingredient not losing its uniqueness in the process, was an exciting, if frustrating, search. People like Alain Locke yearned for a workable union on equal terms for both races. He respected and believed in the American ideals at the same time that he respected and believed in the uniqueness of the black man and his experiences in America. The fact that an exciting implementation of cultural pluralism was not achieved for black Americans does not diminish the efforts of those black writers who devoted themselves to its pursuit. One of the many unfortunate ironies that black writers had to face, however, was the view taken by racists that it was the difference of black people that demanded their eternal subservience. Difference can also mean inferiority. White southerners had always claimed that blacks were biologically and culturally different from white people as their justification for separatism. Now, black writers were claiming separatism as a desired goal. The positions had become muddled.

A study of black intellectual reformers also raises serious questions about how change can be effected in this country. The critic-reformers whom we have discussed can be divided into two basic categories: those whom I would label "conventional" critics, namely those who attack the hypocrisy of white America but not the fundamental value system; and those whom I would call "radical" critics, those who repudiated the value system. DuBois, Kelly Miller, Frazier, and most of the men described in this study, would be in the first category. Langston Hughes's critique of white American culture and the Garvey and Marxist critiques would be radical responses. Is it not possible to imagine that "conventional" critics, after many years, would begin to reexamine their methods *and* goals and wonder how meaningful they are? If a "conventional" critic finds himself impotent, if he finds that the approved methodology does not achieve the desired results, would it not be logical to think that he would reevaluate his methods and possibly his goals?

W. E. B. DuBois's discussion of boycotts and collective action in the early 1930s could be viewed as an effort to adapt and change the methodology of reform to the changing conditions. His goals did not change, but his means to attain them did. Would not this stage in the career of a devoted (and long-lived) reformer be followed, almost naturally, by a rejection of both the goals and methods of the system when no significant changes resulted from continuous and honest effort? It seems quite logical and understandable that a "conventional" critic would eventually become a "radical" critic. Democratic capitalism would then be replaced with democratic socialism; propaganda, pressure tactics, and ameliorative legislation would be abandoned for direct action, violence, and guerrilla tactics. Most reformers remain amazingly dogged in their loyalty to a philosophy and program; but the long career of W. E. B. DuBois dramatically reflects that after forty years' devotion to the American system, serious questioning of it resulted in an abandonment of it. DuBois never gave up his belief in democracy; but he gave up believing that it could be achieved in the United States. Given the evidence, it would be difficult to fault him for this judgment.

*   *   *

The major questions concerning race relations were asked, often eloquently, during the first thirty years of this century. How can white Americans preach equality and practice inequality? In what ways can both races participate in the American Dream? Is biracial harmony a feasible goal? What are the best methods for achieving peaceful and meaningful change? Many black writers also provided answers to these questions. They often devoted their lives to the cause of civil rights. They tried, in their daily efforts through organizations such as the NAACP and the Urban League, as well as through their writings, to create positive and nonviolent change in race relations. Their failure must be viewed as the failure of the American Dream, not as their personal failure. To the overwhelming majority of black writers during the years 1900–1930, the future not only appeared brighter, but also assured success. The success did not come during the next forty years although significant positive changes did occur. It is left to the descendants of those writers, in the final thirty years of this century, to carry on their legacy and to bridge the gap between American ideals and American reality for black Americans.

Bibliographical Essay

As the Preface and the footnotes throughout suggest, this study relied heavily upon the magazine literature of the period. Footnote citations can be consulted for amplification of the quotations and interpretations presented therein. The writings of key black leaders such as Booker T. Washington, W. E. B. DuBois, and James Weldon Johnson also provide important additional information on black thought. Washington's *Up From Slavery* (New York, 1901), for example, is a classic example of the success story genre, an important component of the American Dream myth. James Weldon Johnson's *Along This Way* (New York, 1933) is also a worthwhile autobiography. His *Autobiography of an Ex-Coloured Man,* anonymously published in 1912 and republished under his name in 1927, is a good fictionalized account of life in the South for a black man. Johnson's *Black Manhattan* (New York, 1930), written within a progressive framework, gave a great deal of information on black theatrical life. DuBois, a most prolific writer, wrote mainly for *Crisis* during this period although his collection of essays, *The Souls of Black Folk* (Chicago, 1903), and his editorship of the *Atlantic University Publications* (1897–1915) brought him to the attention of black and white America; the latter series, moreover, has a wealth of information on the black community. Additional autobiographies worth consulting are Claude McKay's *Home to Harlem* (New York, 1928) and Langston Hughes's *The Big Sea: An Autobiography* (New York, 1940). Less well-known but important is William Pickens's *Bursting Bonds* (Boston, 1929).

Crisis, Opportunity, and the *Messenger* have all been reprinted by Negro Universities Press (New York, 1969) as part of their series, Negro Periodicals in the United States, 1840–1960. The *Southern Workman* is less accessible. Very few university or public libraries have it. In addition to the black periodicals, however, two "white" magazines devoted a good deal of space to the Negro problem. *Survey,* the official magazine of social workers, in its March, 1925, issue, for example, became the basis for the book, *The New Negro* (New York, 1925), edited by Alain Locke. The *Annals of the American Academy of Political and Social Science* also had whole issues on the black American; one of the most noteworthy was the November, 1928, issue which offered a comprehensive view of the black American's status.

Contemporary studies, written during the 1900–1930 period or shortly thereafter, that remain valuable works are: Herbert Seligmann's *The Negro Faces America* (New York, 1920); Ray Stannard Baker's *Following the Color Line* (New York, 1908; reprinted, New York, 1964); Mary White Ovington's *Half a Man: The Status of the Negro in New York* (New York, 1911); Sterling D. Spero and Abram L. Harris's *The Black Worker* (New York, 1931); Kelly Miller's *Race Adjustment* (3d ed., New York, 1910); Thomas J. Woofter's *Negro Migration* (New York, 1920); and Emmett J. Scott's *Negro Migration During the War* (New York, 1920). After the race riot of 1919 in Chicago, a commission was formed to investigate the causes and recommend some solutions to the race problem. Their findings, published in 1922, remain an important and relevant statement: the Chicago Commission on Race Relations, *The Negro in Chicago* (Chicago, 1922).

The best general survey of black Americans for all time periods is John Hope Franklin's *From Slavery to Freedom* (2d ed., New York, 1956). A more specialized interpretive study that provides important information on the life of black southerners and white attitudes toward them is C. Vann Woodward's *Origins of the New South, 1877–1913* (Baton Rouge, 1951). Woodward's *The Strange Career of Jim Crow* (rev. ed., New York, 1965) also gives the reader a brief but thoughtful view of segregation. George B. Tindall's *The*

Emergence of the New South, 1913–1945 (Baton Rouge, 1967) is a very detailed description of life and thought in the white South with some significant information on black Americans as well. Gilbert Osofsky's *Harlem: The Making of a Ghetto* (New York, 1963) and Allan Spear's *Black Chicago: The Making of a Negro Ghetto, 1890–1920* (Chicago, 1967) are detailed discussions of those respective black communities. Black sociologists E. Franklin Frazier's *The Negro Family in the United States* (Chicago, 1939) and Charles S. Johnson's *Shadow of the Plantation* (Chicago, 1934) also provide important data on the life of black Americans in the early years of this century. Gunner Myrdal's classic *An American Dilemma: The Negro Problem and Modern Democracy* (New York, 1944) is still the most comprehensive overview of the subject and one in which the issue is posed in terms of the American value system and its promises to all Americans.

Additional specialized studies worth consulting include: Louis R. Harlan, *Separate and Unequal: Public School Campaigns and Racism in the Southern Seaboard States, 1901–1915* (Chapel Hill, 1958); V. O. Key, *Southern Politics in State and Nation* (New York, 1949); Harold F. Gosnell, *Negro Politicians: The Rise of Negro Politics in Chicago* (Chicago, 1935); James Q. Wilson, *Negro Politics: The Search for Leadership* (Glencoe, Ill., 1960); Benjamin E. Mays and Joseph W. Nicholson, *The Negro's Church* (New York, 1933); and a good collection of documents, *Negro Protest Thought in the Twentieth Century*, edited by Francis L. Broderick and August Meier (Indianapolis, 1966).

The black poets, short story writers, and novelists included in this study were those most often mentioned by the black press. By necessity, the work included was very selective; only a small portion of those novels, stories, and poems that related to the American Dream theme were discussed. The Negro Universities Press (Westport, Connecticut) is currently reprinting many of the Harlem Renaissance novels of the 1920s in a readable, compact form. A new study of the Renaissance by Nathan Huggins, *Harlem Renaissance* (New York, 1971), has just been published. Benjamin Brawley's *The Negro in Literature and Art in the United States* (New York, 1939), Sterling Brown's *The Negro in American Fiction* (Washington, D.C., 1937), and Robert Bone's *The Negro Novel in America* (New Haven, 1958) are decent surveys of the subject.

The literature on black radicalism is not as extensive as the reader would desire. Marcus Garvey received the most attention in the contemporary periodicals of the day. Edmund David Cronon's *Black Moses: The Story of Marcus Garvey and the Universal Negro Improvement Association* (Madison, Wis., 1955), although a cursory overview, remains the only summary of Garvey's life and career. No biography has been written on A. Philip Randolph or many of the other black radicals of the period. Indeed, a thorough analysis of black intellectual leadership has yet to be written. Harold Cruse's *The Crisis of the Negro Intellectual: From Its Origin to the Present* (New York, 1967) is an interesting work but its polemical and one-sided nature limits its worth. Wilson Record's *The Negro and the Communist Party* (Chapel Hill, 1951) is a helpful study, as are Jack Greenberg's *Race Relations and American Law* (New York, 1959); Herbert Garfinkel's *When Negroes March: The March on Washington Movement in the Organizational Politics for FEPC* (Glencoe, Ill., 1959); and Clement E. Vose's *Caucasians Only: The Supreme Court, the NAACP and the Restrictive Covenant Cases* (Berkeley, 1959). The two biographies of W. E. B. DuBois are Francis L. Broderick, *W. E. B. DuBois: Negro Leader in Time of Crisis* (Stanford, 1959); and Elliott M. Rudwick, *W. E. B. DuBois: A Study in Minority Group Leadership* (Philadelphia, 1960).

Index